DATE DUE

A FINE WILL BE CHARGED FOR EACH OVERDUE MATERIAL.

Doris Betts

Twayne's United States Authors Series

Frank Day, Editor

Clemson University

TUSAS 689

DORIS WAUGH BETTS
Staff photograph, Communications Division, Georgia Institute of Technology, Atlanta, Georgia.

Doris Betts

Elizabeth Evans

Georgia Institute of Technology

Twayne Publishers
An Imprint of Simon & Schuster Macmillan
New York

Prentice Hall International
London • Mexico City • New Delhi • Singapore • Sydney • Toronto

Twayne's United States Authors Series No. 689

Doris Betts
Elizabeth Evans

Copyright © 1997 by Twayne Publishers

Twayne Publishers
An Imprint of Simon & Schuster Macmillan
1633 Broadway
New York, NY 10019

Library of Congress Cataloging-in-Publication Data

Evans, Elizabeth, 1935–
    Doris Betts / Elizabeth Evans.
        p.   cm. — (Twayne's United States authors series ; TUSAS 689)
    Includes bibliographical references and index.
    ISBN 0-8057-7826-8 (alk. paper)
    1. Betts, Doris—Criticism and interpretation.   2. Women and
literature—Southern States—History—20th century.   I. Title.
II. Series.
PS3552.E84Z65   1997
813'.54—dc21   97-21416
                                                           CIP

10 9 8 7 6 5 4 3 2

Printed in the United States of America

For
Louise Hardeman Abbot
royal friend

Contents

Preface   *ix*
Acknowledgments   *xi*
Chronology   *xiii*

Chapter One
The Many Threads of One Life   1

Chapter Two
One Woman's Intriguing Mind: A Life of
Writing and the Story Collections   37

Chapter Three
Better Failures: The First Three Novels   60

Chapter Four
Heading West and East: The Later Three Novels   78

Chapter Five
Private Self—Public Life   99

Notes and References   *109*
Selected Bibliography   *127*
Index   *135*

Preface

Since 1953 Doris Betts has been writing and publishing—six novels and three collections of short stories to date. Without question, her list of titles would be longer if she had not chosen to teach and to maintain a most active public life. Although Betts at times envies writers who have a more private lifestyle, she herself has been an active figure on the campus of the University of North Carolina at Chapel Hill for over 30 years. With no undergraduate degree, Betts rose from lecturer (1966) to Alumni Distinguished Professor of English (1980). She has won the University of North Carolina's awards for distinguished teaching and delights in that teaching because, she says, it keeps the arteries from hardening. She has directed the freshman-sophomore English program, directed the honors program and the Fellows program, and has been named to numerous posts of responsibility including chair of the faculty, the first woman to hold that office. Her contributions to the university and to the state of North Carolina have been recognized by her colleagues and her neighbors, as well as by the governor and the legislature.

The list of "miscellaneous speeches" fills two pages in Betts's vita, and the audiences are diverse: from a retreat for Time-Life editors to the North Carolina Medical Auxiliary, from the American Writers Congress in New York to the First Presbyterian Church in Durham. She has spoken to students and faculty at over 50 colleges and universities from Central Carolina Technical Institute to West Point Military Academy. Her articles and essays have appeared in a wide range of publications from *Life* to *North Carolina Education,* from the *Presbyterian Outlook* to the *South Atlantic Quarterly.* Her short stories have appeared in more than 25 magazines and journals and have been included in over 25 anthologies. Her book reviews appear in newspapers of North Carolina, as well as in the *Washington Post Book World,* the *New York Times Book Review,* and the *Los Angeles Times.*

She maintains a busy, if not frenetic, schedule, surviving because she has boundless energy and is careful never to stand in line. She shares with her major female characters a determination to press on with life, to avoid being victimized in any way, and to pursue, not happiness, but cheerfulness. Her characters are generally blue-collar, middle-class, and not college educated—the kind of people she came from in the Piedmont section of North Carolina. Although some characters are professionals, Betts's attention often centers on those whose limited education precludes their discussing philosophical matters. Nevertheless, they *do* wonder and worry about profound things—time, love, change, mortality. "A writer's duty," Betts says, "is to put into words what it is like to be a human being in this world, even for the inarticulate."

Although the Piedmont section of North Carolina has given Betts both place and people, as novelist she continues to broaden the locale, moving to the West for the major action in *Heading West* and in *The Sharp Teeth of Love*. Indeed, in the latter novel, Betts sets one scene in Italy. And although she firmly resists being labeled a "Christian writer," Betts calls herself a writer who is a Christian. "Faith," Betts says, "is the decision to keep your eyes open or, as Walker Percy might say, 'to be on to something.' " Betts continues to be "on to something," and the basis of her work evolves from the deep influences of the region where she grew up and from her strong early training in the Associate Reformed Presbyterian Church. Many readers catch the biblical allusions in Betts's work but miss the strong theological tenets that are also present. She shares with the late Walker Percy the notion that the end of art is knowledge, and that knowledge, as Percy's biographer, Jay Tolson, points out, is "knowledge of the Christian message." Both Percy and Betts convey the "good news" of the gospel without compromising artistic standards.

Betts is not, and does not try to be, a didactic writer, and she says that like Kierkegaard, she has not been called as an apostle. Fiction rarely, if ever, alters circumstances or reality, Betts contends, but it can "speak the truth to people who hear it. And that's quite sufficient." Her novels and short stories reflect her considerable comic ability, include sexual encounters, depict adventure, and explore the terrors and triumphs of the very young and the very old. Hers is work from a well-read author who uses allusions with skill and creates characters that readers remember.

In his 1996 biography *Charles Ives: A Life with Music*, Jan Swafford argues that to Ives music was not abstract in its essence but instead "something people do for the benefit of people." Doris Betts would certainly say that writing good short stories and novels is indeed "something people do for the benefit of people."

Acknowledgments

I am grateful to William J. Kirwan, university librarian, Western Carolina University, for library privileges and courtesies.

I owe thanks to Mrs. Margie Wessels and to other staff members of the Iredell County Public Library, Statesville, North Carolina.

I am grateful to Chandler Gordon of the Captain's Bookshelf, Asheville, North Carolina, for his generous help.

I am grateful to Noelle Kehrberg and particularly to Nina Marable for such patient help with this project.

I am grateful to Alice Cotten of the North Carolina Collection, Wilson Library, University of North Carolina at Chapel Hill, for her library assistance and for reading portions of this manuscript.

I thank Barbara Habel Hyde, Professor David L. Walker, Professor William L. Andrews, and James Deveroux, S.J., for permission to quote from their correspondence to Doris Betts.

Lee Smith and Joseph M. Flora kindly granted me interviews and also permitted me to quote from them. I am most grateful to both for their time and interest.

For their great courtesy and assistance during my research visits, I am grateful to Dr. Howard Gotlieb, director, and to Margaret Goostray of the Mugar Memorial Library, Boston University. Dr. Gotlieb has kindly granted me permission to quote from the Doris Betts Collection.

I am, as always, grateful to Professor Frank Day, Clemson University, for his straightforward and helpful editorial advice.

I owe thanks to Louise Hardeman Abbot for making available her correspondence from Doris Betts, for reading portions of this manuscript, and for her indispensable encouragement.

Finally, I owe thanks to Doris Waugh Betts for permission to quote from her correspondence and from the Doris Betts Collection, Mugar Memorial Library, Boston University. I thank her, too, for keeping her early pledge "to offer, simultaneously: (1) all help possible and (2) no meddling." She has indeed offered all help possible—and then some. Meddling is not a Bettsian trait.

Chronology

1932	Doris June (Waugh) Betts born 4 June in Iredell County, North Carolina, the only child of William Elmore and Mary Ellen (Freeze) Waugh.
1946–1950	Works part-time on *Statesville Daily Record.*
1950	Graduates from Statesville High School.
1950–1953	Enters University of North Carolina, Greensboro (Woman's College); leaves without earning a degree.
1950–1957	Works as stringer for UPI and various North Carolina newspapers.
1952	Marries Lowry Matthews Betts, a law student, who retires from his legal career in 1997 as district judge of Chatham and Orange Counties, North Carolina.
1953	Awarded Phi Beta Kappa; wins *Mademoiselle* College Fiction Contest for "Mr. Shawn and Father Scott" (included in *Best Short Stories of 1953*); daughter Doris LewEllyn born; family moves to Chapel Hill.
1953–1954	Works part-time on *Chapel Hill Weekly.*
1954	Wins UNC-Putnam Booklength Manuscript Prize for *The Gentle Insurrection and Other Stories;* teaches typing for North Carolina Highway Patrol; son David Lowry born.
1955–1957	Works as office manager and secretary-treasurer for Simplified Farm Record Book Company (advertising, printing) in Chapel Hill.
1957	Family moves to Sanford, North Carolina; Lowry Betts joins law firm of Pittman and Staton; publishes first novel, *Tall Houses in Winter.*
1957–1958	Works full-time as feature writer and daily columnist for *Sanford Daily Herald.*
1958	Wins Sir Walter Raleigh Award.
1958–1959	Awarded Guggenheim Fellowship in Creative Writing.

1958–1960   Serves on editorial board of *N. C. Democrat.*

1960   Works as full-time editor, Sanford *News Leader;* son Erskine Moore born.

1962–1964   Serves on North Carolina Tercentenary Commission.

1964   *The Scarlet Thread.*

1965   Wins Sir Walter Raleigh Award.

1965   *The Astronomer and Other Stories.*

1966–1974   Joins English Department, University of North Carolina at Chapel Hill, as lecturer.

1970   *Creative Writing: The Short Story* (textbook for correspondence course, extension division, University of North Carolina at Chapel Hill.)

1971   Is visiting lecturer in creative writing at Duke University; makes first trip to Grand Canyon.

1972   *The River to Pickle Beach.*

1972–1978   Serves as director of Freshman-Sophomore English, University of North Carolina at Chapel Hill.

1973   *Beasts of the Southern Wild and Other Stories* is finalist for the National Book Award; wins Tanner Award for distinguished undergraduate teaching; wins Sir Walter Raleigh Award.

1974   Promoted to associate professor, University of North Carolina at Chapel Hill.

1975   North Carolina Award for Literature from North Carolina Legislature.

1975–1976   Named director of North Carolina Fellows Program, University of North Carolina at Chapel Hill.

1978   Promoted to professor, University of North Carolina at Chapel Hill; named to National Humanities Faculty.

1978–1980   Serves on Literature Panel, National Endowment for the Arts, chair 1979–1980.

1978–1981   Named assistant dean, Honors Program, University of North Carolina at Chapel Hill.

1980   Named Alumni Distinguished Professor, University of North Carolina at Chapel Hill; wins Katherine Carmichael Award for teaching; inducted into Golden Fleece, University of North Carolina at Chapel Hill; moves with husband to Araby Farm, Pittsboro, North Carolina.

1981   *Heading West. Violet,* film version of "The Ugliest Pilgrim," wins Academy Award for Best Short Feature; wins Special Grand Jury Award, Houston Film Festival.

1981–1984   Serves on Board of Governors, University of North Carolina Press.

1982–1985   Elected chair of the faculty, University of North Carolina at Chapel Hill.

1983   Wins John Dos Passos Award; wins Distinguished Service Award for Women (Chi Omega).

1984   Serves as judge PEN-Faulkner Awards.

1985   *3 by 3. Masterpieces of the Southern Gothic (Beasts of the Southern Wild).*

1986   Named a Celebrated Teacher by the Association of Departments of English, Modern Language Association; University of North Carolina at Chapel Hill English Department establishes Doris Betts Teaching Award; serves as consultant to Southern Growth Policies Board and writes their report, *Halfway Home and a Long Way To Go.*

1987   Nominated as candidate for chancellor, University of North Carolina at Chapel Hill.

1988   Serves as consultant to Florida Forestry Commission and writes report, *Turning Over a New Leaf.*

1988–1989   Named chair, Committee on Athletics and the University, University of North Carolina at Chapel Hill.

1989   Awarded Medal of Merit in the Short Story, American Academy and Institute of Arts and Letters; wins Salem Award for Literary Achievement; awarded honorary degree, University of North Carolina at Greensboro.

1991   Wins R. Hunt Parker Memorial Award, North Carolina Literary and Historical Association for literary achievement; wins University of North Carolina Alumni Award for distinguished teaching.

1992   Selected for the John Tyler Caldwell Award, North
        Carolina Humanities Committee; named faculty direc-
        tor, University of North Carolina Publishing Institute;
        named to Board of Trustees, Union Theological Semi-
        nary, Richmond, Virginia; named to Board of Trustees,
        National Humanities Center; elected to Fellowship of
        Southern Writers.

1994   *Souls Raised from the Dead;* named on *New York Times* list
        of 20 best books for 1994.

1995   Wins Southern Book Award, Southern Book Critics
        Circle.

1997   *Violet,* a musical based on "The Ugliest Pilgrim," opens
        in New York; *The Sharp Teeth of Love.*

Chapter One
The Many Threads of One Life

The honor of "senior superlatives" bestowed upon high school class-mates may not accurately predict future success, but the 1950 graduating class of Statesville (North Carolina) High School hit the mark when they selected Doris Waugh as "Most Talented." Four years later, Doris Waugh Betts had published her first book, *The Gentle Insurrection and Other Stories*, which won the UNC-Putnam prize. By 1978 Betts was the first woman named full professor in the University of North Carolina Department of English (historically not hospitable to women faculty). By 1980 Betts was named Alumni Distinguished Professor of English at the University of North Carolina, her rise remarkable because she did not earn an undergraduate degree. The university, in its wisdom, broke precedent, recognizing and rewarding "professional competency."

Betts's life, as one critic has suggested, makes a "Hortense" Alger story.[1] Her parents, William Elmore and Mary Ellen Freeze Waugh, grew up in North Carolina on Iredell County farms and in early married life worked in a Statesville cotton mill. Although not raised in a bookish family, Betts's father could describe the ordinary events of a day in vivid terms; Betts remembers his speaking with an enthusiasm that transformed the mundane into something altogether exciting.

Only recently has Betts recounted the poignant story of William Elmore Waugh, born out of wedlock to one Daisy Cloninger, who named him for her father and raised the child to age four—when the money ran out. She then made an arrangement with a childless farm couple who came in the middle of the night to claim the sleeping child. (He was never legally adopted by the Waughs.) The four-year-old boy woke up in a strange room amid strangers who "gave him jar lids to play with."[2] Small wonder that as he grew he developed a stutter and a temper. Hoping an old wives' tale was true, his stepmother attempted to cure the stutter by breaking a cake of hot corn bread over the child's head. What heat and crumbs failed to remedy, time healed.

Secure in an "adopted" son and farmworker, the Waughs suddenly began producing children of their own—a total of four redheaded siblings whose appearance clashed sharply with William Elmore's coal

1

black hair and dark eyes. Nevertheless, they all adjusted into relative ease on the farm, until the day when William's stepmother called him in to wash his hands before entering the front room to meet his *"real mother"* ("Daisy," 271). It is no wonder that his stuttering returned. Yet he survived it all, made a happy marriage, produced a singularly remarkable daughter, and in the end faithfully cared for both mothers, mourning each as she died.

When William Elmore Waugh died in 1983, a distant relative sent Betts a photograph of Daisy Cloninger Turner. She is 15, not yet pregnant by the traveling salesman from Greensboro. Captured in the static world of photography, "she stands there forever—and stands there for no time at all, . . . young and beautiful in her pure white dress. She looks like me," Betts writes. "Her very dark eyes look like mine, like my children's" ("Daisy," 273).

Both of Betts's parents encouraged her interest in books, and her father in particular took delight in providing books, once buying a used bookcase for five dollars filled with an inexpensive encyclopedia flanked by novels of Zane Grey, Edgar Rice Burroughs, and Charles Alden Seltzer. Considering cowboy stories suspect, Betts's mother (a member of the conservative Associate Reformed Presbyterian Church) asked from time to time if Betts were finding any bad words between the gaudy covers of the Western novels. With the quick wit that would come to characterize her personality and her writing, Betts replied, "No ma'am, and if I come to any, I'll skip 'em."

While Betts was still too young to stay alone, her mother used the Statesville Public Library as a free baby-sitter when she had shopping errands. Instantly in her element, Betts's delight increased when she "learned to cut through the employees' bathrooms to the adult section."[3] Watchful librarians would not let children check out adult books, but they could read away undisturbed. When she gave the 1981 commencement address at Mitchell Community College in her hometown, Betts recalled her early love affair with the library. The scar still shows on one knee, she told her audience, "which tore open on a chain link fence behind Mitchell College as I cut through from the tall houses on Walnut Street . . . to reach [the] Statesville Public Library, because I believed then that anyone ought to pass dragons or overcome obstacles on the way to the wonderful kingdom of books."[4] Betts's early reading also included "big little books," fat volumes that sold for 49¢ at J. C. Penney. By the time Betts was a second grader, the extended family caught on that Doris was "a reader," and her "farmer kinfolk—who measured literature, like meat, by the pound—were giving me Walter Scott and Dickens."[5]

Far more important to Betts than the cowboys and the classics, however, was a volume called "Story of the Bible for Young and Old," a profusely illustrated book that the Reverend Jesse Lyman Hurlbut, D.D., first copyrighted in 1904. Between its covers were 757 pages retelling 168 stories, "running," the frontispiece claimed, "from Genesis to Revelation" ("Reading," 1G). It was a door-to-door salesman who offered the leather-bound copy of Hurlbut, and Betts's mother gave him a sale, putting down $5 of hard-earned cotton mill money and paying off the $11 price at $1 a week. Hurlbut's stories arrived for Betts's fifth birthday.

More than 50 years later, Betts spotted a used book on the shelf of a Chapel Hill bookstore. Even though the color was wrong and the book now seemed less heavy, Betts recognized Hurlbut straightaway, a moment that called up childhood memories of reading from that birthday gift. The stories retold in Hurlbut prepared Betts for the biblical allusions threading their way throughout Western literature, resonating connections and levels of meaning, and for a lifelong association with the King James Bible and the church. Betts's sophistication places her in the company of theologians—she has been a trustee of Union Theological Seminary in Richmond, Virginia.

At age five, Betts learned from Hurlbut's pages "that individuals mattered, their biographies were significant." Strangely yet profoundly yoked with Hurlbut were those cowboy stories from which, Betts says, she learned "a love of action, landscape, animals; a preference for the kind of protagonist who takes things into his own hands. The pull between these two literatures can be seen in almost everything I have written since" ("Reading," 5G).

During her childhood, Betts enjoyed the farm life of her kin, particularly her grandfather, whose life was attuned to the cycles of nature. John Guy Freeze, her maternal grandfather, gave little heed to Betts's early dreams of becoming a writer: "Let me know when you make 110 on arithmetic," he'd say, because unlike the intricate mystery of words, arithmetic was a "real subject."[6] In her article "My Grandfather Haunts This Farm," published in the *Saturday Evening Post,* Betts recounts her childhood pleasure when she drew her grandfather's name at Christmas time—a scaled-down arrangement for gift giving that many families use when money is tight. Her selection, a $4.95 white shirt from J. C. Penney, served not as part of her grandfather's Sunday church outfit, but ironically as part of his burial clothes. A stroke felled the old man, and as he waited upon death, family members visited one at a time. When his granddaughter's turn came, she asked the question the living helplessly pose to the dying: "How are you feeling?"

His response brought no sign of light or angels or the heavenly host. He pulled his hand from beneath the sheet and said, "with my fingers" ("Grandfather," 86). The literal joke, juxtaposed with impending death, faintly echoes Dylan Thomas's plea that his own father "Rage, rage against the dying of the light." When he died, Betts's grandfather was 85, she 11. His presence lingers for Betts, ghostlike, across the 80 acres of the farm where she now lives. His presence enters the pages of her fiction as Angus Mackey in *The Scarlet Thread,* where the young granddaughter, Esther Allen, watches over his death alone. Nancy Finch in *Heading West* harbors deep memories of her grandfather, dead long before the action of the novel begins. Of all her family, only he forced Nancy to risk the difficult and the frightening. In *Souls Raised from the Dead,* Dandy Thompson tells banal jokes that help him to disguise his fears and insecurities and to survive the severest of tests when his young granddaughter, Mary Grace, dies.

Perhaps the most moving account of John Guy Freeze is in an early (and uncollected) story, "The End of Summer."[7] No death scene occurs, but there is the pain of parting when the granddaughter Mary ends her stay on the farm, returning with her parents and their new baby to life in the city. What Betts conveys is the unspoken—and unspeakable—love the old man has for Mary. As he watches, the child—finally heeding her grandmother's calls for supper—comes into view. As she does, "he felt his heart lift slightly and turn once and settle back" (9). No one, Anne Tyler declares in her review of Betts's collection, *Beasts of the Southern Wild,*[8] writes about love better than Doris Betts. Often that love radiates between the very old and the very young.

Fingerprints of Style

When asked about the origins of her fiction, Betts quickly names the source as "Bible stories, beyond question." Those wonderful stories function far beyond the narrative line because "they make the place where you live nontemporal; it is always possible that if an angel showed up on the threshing floor, appearances could happen anywhere. It makes you feel that the ordinary is not ordinary."[9]

Betts's mother, a faithful churchgoer, finally prevailed, and her husband, too, joined the Associate Reformed Presbyterian Church (eventually serving as Sunday school teacher, elder, and church treasurer), whose initials, A.R.P., Mrs. Waugh often declares stand for "All Right People." (In *The Sharp Teeth of Love*, Betts makes a minor character a member of the A.R.P. church.) Although a shrinking body numbering between 20,000 and 30,000,[10] the denomination remains today quite conservative, Betts says. "There are no women elders, much less ministers. They still speak of homosexuality as a sin, period. There are no gradations. There's no place to move from; you're either in or you're out. They remain everything that I both loathed and benefited from simultaneously" (Ketchin, 242).

There were benefits from the denomination's educated clergy, an informed knowledge of the Scriptures and a profound love of the psalms. Children learned and recited the Longer and the Shorter Catechisms, memorized Scripture, and took part in "sword drills" to demonstrate their ability to recite Bible verses word for word. Betts often remarks that the hours she spent in church services each week match the hours her own children spent watching television.

These positive features, however, do not diminish the A.R.P.'s "standard Calvinist bent," and Betts argues that the doctrine of the elect has an "ugly truth" illustrated in the biblical prediction that the sins of the fathers will be visited upon the third and fourth generations. It's clearly in evidence, Betts says. "If you're a drunk, those children are penalized by it, or if you're a child abuser you've passed it on; and to that degree, . . . there is an almost genetic predestination. Sometimes an environmental one. Americans as a rule think everything can be fixed, but I don't think that" (Ketchin, 242–43).

Although for a time Betts abandoned the church, variously describing herself as an "unaffiliated Theist" or on occasion an "agnostic," the early training remained in her metaphoric ear. Echoes from Hurlbut and sounds of the King James Bible are never absent from her fiction. Occasionally, characters' names (Esther, Thomas, David in *The Scarlet Thread*) echo biblical, and biblical allusion comes as easily—and almost as frequently—to Betts as breathing. Long returned to the established church (Presbyterian now), Betts speaks of her compelling interest in theodicy, the problem of vindicating divine goodness in the midst of evil and the seemingly unmerited suffering people bear. It is this paradox Betts explores in *Souls Raised from the Dead*.

From her active role in church matters today, Betts still bristles occasionally over John Calvin, appalled to learn in a biography that Calvin's only comment at his wife's funeral was " 'She never interfered with my work.' Wouldn't you like to go back through history and whip the man?" Betts demanded of her interviewer (Ketchin, 244). One of Betts's works in progress, a novel called *The Wings of the Morning* (the title from Psalm 139), has characters who are members of the Associate Reformed Presbyterian Church. An image in this manuscript suggests the difficult theological paradox under which Betts has ironically thrived. "The denomination leaned toward theocracy, yet had such joy in singing the Psalms, and such a generous doctrinal view of God's grace that, like an Alpine floral mat, these colored with surprises the colder heights of Calvinism."[11]

This religious milieu and the landscape and mores of her southern Piedmont North Carolina have formed what Betts as writer calls her "fingerprints of style." Her hometown of Statesville lies near the center of North Carolina in Iredell County, a place far removed from plantation memories and remnants of slavery. No *Gone with the Wind* myths prevail; instead, blue-collar workers, farmers, and middle-class businesspeople live and work there, people like those who constitute Betts's fictional world. Born in 1932, Betts grew up on the cusp of the depression aware that nobody she really knew got everything they wanted because cash was scarce. Betts describes her early years living near mill housing on the wrong side of the tracks as a lean, but not a seriously deprived, time. "We ate well," she recalls. "You didn't eat 'rich,' but you ate well."[12]

Southern small-town life in the 1930s and 1940s survived hard economic times as well as the sacrifices World War II required, and that life—at least publicly—was church centered and deeply patriotic. It was a time when the South voted the Democratic ticket—straight—when divorce was scarcely heard of and caused scandal when it happened. Boy Scout news made the front page of the local paper, which also periodically ran the school honor rolls. Most businesses bore the names of their local owners—Lazenby-Montgomery Hardware, Sherrill-White Shoe Company—and in those pretelevision years, the Statesville newspaper ran a weekly radio schedule particularly noting special musical programs. It was a time when even short trips made the news. ("Mrs. Pegram Bryant went to Charlotte [38 miles distant] to spend a few days with Mrs. W. M. Robey.") Children's birthday parties were reported with guests' names listed and refreshments described. A highlight for Statesville in May 1929 was a seven-day visit of the Redpath Chautauqua, featuring the dramatic soprano Lorna Doone Jackson.

Small southern town readers followed regional and national reports of projects begun by the federal Works Progress Authority, which provided jobs for thousands during and after the depression. And these same readers, hoping war would not reach them, may well have taken temporary comfort in such headlines as "Roosevelt Says This Nation Will Protect Herself but Aggression on Part of U.S. Impossibility: Neighborliness Is the Watchword." The outbreak of World War II, however, was not averted by the watchword "neighborliness," and the paper soon printed in its columns the names of local men called up for the draft.

In 1942 (when Betts was 10 years old) the Rationing Board began operation in Statesville. Books of stamps were issued to families, and only if the proper stamp accompanied the money could a person buy goods in short supply—shoes, gasoline, tires, and many food items. Even the sales of Coca-Cola, that southern standby, were restricted. In newspaper advertisements, businesses encouraged conservation and patriotism. Troutman's Auto Service, for instance, told people to SAVE YOUR TIRES. Lazenby-Montgomery Hardware urged people to bring in small appliances and tools for repair because, their ad continued, "War Must Change the Easy-Going American Way." L. Gordon Iron and Metal Company's ad called out to the public: "Attention! America Needs Iron-Metal-Paper and Rags to Win the War." Women met to sew for the Red Cross, families planted victory gardens, and when medical doctors between the ages of 20 and 45 were called up for the draft, Iredell County was left in 1942 with one doctor for 4,800 people.

Throughout the country women were recruited to replace men in war industries and plants; the era of "Rosie the Riveter" had arrived. But women who remained at home were also expected to contribute to the war effort, especially in drives to collect fat (needed to produce certain medicines), paper, rags, and clothes. (The local Rotary Club ran a photograph of war refugees with the caption "What can *you* spare that they can wear?") The Department of Agriculture addressed women in the kitchen: "What Can I Do? Lady, You Can *Can!*" Vegetables from victory gardens supplied the summer table, and many women did can the excess, putting the jars by for the winter months. The marines began to enlist 17-year-old boys, bootlegging in stolen tires was widespread, and many hoarded food. The war years were upon the country, and upon Statesville as well.

Nevertheless, ordinary life continued. Amid the war headlines, battle reports, and casualty lists, the local paper reported social events—dances, bridal luncheons, birthday parties. And most North Carolinians clung to their radios for the 1943 Rose Bowl broadcast because Duke played Oregon (in Durham), losing 20 to 16. Unaware of the full impact of war news, children could turn to the comics—Dr. Bobbs, Little Orphan Annie, Etta Kett, Popeye. (Along with Popeye's exploits, Betts may well have remembered a 1942 headline in the Statesville paper—"Nazi Submarines Are Raiding Ships within 100 Miles of New York"—and much later remembered this alarming report to prompt the fear of two little girls in her autobiographical story set in the war years, "The Spies in the Herb House.") During early 1942, Statesville's picture shows (as movie theaters were called then) showed films with war themes—*Johnny Doughboy* and *Mrs. Miniver* (which won the Academy Award for Best Picture)—as well as the sentimental classic *Lassie Come Home*.

As late as 1944, war bond rallies were critical. Children bought savings stamps and pasted them in special folders until the total reached $18.75—the amount needed to buy a $25.00 war bond. The tone of newspaper announcements indicates that positive responses were all but demanded: "Every American will be asked to invest at least $100 in extra War Bonds. *At least* $100. Better $200, $300, $500. You Can Afford It." A regular column called "With the Colors" reported news of men and women in the armed services and sometimes news of local men who were, in that haunting phrase, "killed somewhere in France."

As World War II drew to its end in 1945, bold headlines of invasions launched and battles won covered the front page of the paper. On other pages, news concentrated on local matters. Churches were calling new ministers, civic and book clubs met, the polio drive was under way, and editorials called for donations to cancer research. Although movies with war themes remained popular, Statesville youngsters were also watching *National Velvet* with Elizabeth Taylor and Mickey Rooney, *Naughty Marietta* with Jeanette MacDonald and Nelson Eddy, and *Laura* with Gene Tierney and Dana Andrews.

In her third novel, *The River to Pickle Beach*, set in 1968, Betts tells the story of Bebe Sellers, who watches reruns on television of the movies she had seen some 20 years ago in her youth. Betts patterned the character Bebe somewhat on her own mother, a moviegoer, who saw many of these 1940s films when the three movie theaters in Statesville were a primary source of entertainment for adults and children.

Details of Statesville are transformed into Betts's fictional Stoneville and Greenway in Stone County, North Carolina; these towns figure prominently in her first three novels. Statesville appears literally as Betts recreates childhood experiences in "All That Glisters Isn't Gold" and

"The Spies in the Herb House." If life in Statesville during the 1930s and 1940s strongly resembles that of countless other small southern towns, it nevertheless was the *place* where Doris Betts grew up. It was a town she gladly left when she was 18, and in late middle age a town she can return to, acknowledging its permanent influence in her life, as she told the 1981 graduating class at Mitchell Community College:

> Now I return to the home town some of you will be leaving, and to BE home, to stand here now, turns me into an Iredell child again. . . . Naturally I have edited the memories of home until mostly good ones remain. I'm one of the last innocents, for instance, convinced that anyone not growing up by the railroad tracks was culturally disadvantaged, because she couldn't wave at the engineer on the Junebug, nor teach herself how to balance the black rail so well she could run on it, arms wide, and never look down at her feet. ("Promises," 1–2)

Education: Making a Life

The lean times in the 1930s, Betts has said, fostered "a work ethic which was very strong at my house and which came also from rural ancestors. Laziness was unforgivable."[13] What Betts describes as nearly inexhaustible energy also figures into the frenetic pace that has marked her life since grammar school. Some University of North Carolina colleagues quip that Betts is not an individual, but an entire department—no *one* person could take on so many tasks, be assigned to so many committees, be elected to so many posts.

Mulberry Street School, where Betts attended grades one to six, included in its student body the children of the mill community. Betts remembers the teachers at this school with gratitude because they were "old-fashioned, stern, believed in memory work, diagraming sentences" and did not hesitate to "pop your palm with a ruler if you didn't behave well" (Ross, 53). Betts remembers, too, that "it gave prestige to fight with people taller than you, and death to admit that you spent your spare hours with books instead of comics"; the "novels" Betts wrote in grammar school were, she claims, "deadlier secrets to me than any I have ever been called upon to keep since that time."[14] Yet Betts credits these grammar school teachers for nurturing a talent they may not have fully recognized. One of them would "say to me, casually, very casually," Betts recalls, " 'I wish someone would write a poem for home room devotional.' " Another just as casually would murmur, "Would you

rather try something a little harder than this? There's a poet called Amy
Lowell . . . a novelist named John Steinbeck" ("Teaching," n.p.). They
"were very demanding teachers," Betts recalls, "who when they found
me idle in school, gave me extra things to do without even a smile. And,
I think, took me seriously."[15]

Her diligence in school stemmed from the Calvinist background that
repeatedly conveyed the message of mortality. " 'Work for the night is
coming.' I just soaked that up from the skin. And I do not regret it. I
think it has been a useful tool" (Powell, 16). Like Flannery O'Connor,
with whom she is often compared, Betts takes the New Testament parable of the talents at face value.

Betts's own high school days were busy with classes, the drama club
(she played a role in *Jane Eyre*), work on the student newspaper, and a
steady stream of part-time jobs. From 1947 to 1950 when she graduated, Betts was, in succession, pianist and record salesman for Bunch's
Music Store, clerk and cashier for Diana Shops,[16] and summer typist for
the local chapter of the American Red Cross; during the entire period,
she was a staff member on the *Statesville Daily Record*. And it was during
her senior year that Betts stepped forward as a writer.[17]

On 22 October 1949, Betts published her first column, "Hitting the
High Spots," in the *Statesville Daily Record* and launched her role as journalist, a role that she continues today. The column appeared weekly,
though not always on the same day of the week, and carried her byline.
When the third column appeared, Betts's photo flanked her name. The
column reported on daily high school activities, but occasionally Betts
took up substantive issues. During this time, Betts also covered the
sports activities, calling in scores late at night to the *Greensboro Daily
News*.

When Betts graduated from high school, she won several awards.
Ironically she did not win the English Medal given by the Kiwanis Club
or the essay contests sponsored by the American War Mothers, the
Woman's Christian Temperance Union, and the American Legion. But
Betts did win a $5 award for being chosen "Girl of the Year," a medal
and a $25 prize from the Civitan Club for her essay on citizenship, a $10
award for outstanding service to the school newspaper, and a typing
medal. She came away with $40 (a princely sum in 1950) and a profi-
ciency in typing that in 1954 led to her teaching a four-week course in
typing (from 7:00 P.M. to 9:00 P.M.) to rookie North Carolina Highway
Patrolmen—62 of them divided into two sections. Years later she would
recall the students in those night classes when she created one of her

most appealing characters, Frank Thompson, a North Carolina Highway Patrolman in *Souls Raised from the Dead*.

A whole new phase of learning began when Betts entered Woman's College (later renamed University of North Carolina–Greensboro) in fall 1950. From her room in Bailey Dormitory, she looked out the window and saw for the first time a real writer, the poet Randall Jarrell, who was on the faculty. At Woman's College, professors set Betts squarely on the path she was to follow. James Painter assessed her writing: the poetry was terrible, the prose might do. Betts remembers fondly her classes with Robie Macauley, and in 1994 Macauley wrote Betts to say that he was buying *Souls Raised from the Dead* and to report that *Tall Houses in Winter* and *The Astronomer and Other Stories* were on his home library shelves. Peter Taylor was another of Betts's professors at Woman's College. In class, Betts recalls, Taylor primarily "read to us things that he was appalled we had not read already. He read them out loud. He was not a particularly dramatic reader. But I don't know that I'd ever been read to that much except in church" (Powell, 16). It was from her writing teacher, Frances Gray Patton (author of *Good Morning, Miss Dove*, 1954), that Betts found both encouragement and example. Patton taught her that "people are always doing something for you and you can't ever pay that person back—so we do for someone else as the opportunity comes."[18] Over the past 30 years, scores of writing students have emerged from Betts's University of North Carolina classes who can, and often do, testify that Betts never failed to seize the opportunity to *do* something.

Betts entered Woman's College intending to study journalism. She was well into her first year before she discovered there was no journalism school and turned to creative writing, an interest quickened by the visits to campus of writers, among them W. H. Auden, Robert Frost, and Robert Penn Warren. When Katherine Anne Porter visited, she critiqued student stories, including Betts's "The Sympathetic Visitor," originally entitled "A Crepe for Her Brother." (The revised story was sold to *Mademoiselle* and then included in Betts's first collection, *The Gentle Insurrection and Other Stories*, 1954.) Porter herself made a lasting impression. Tiny, with brilliant white hair, Porter swept into a cocktail party and lit a cigarette. All the young men flew to her side, ready to catch a falling ash, leaving Betts and the other young women to stand aside and watch Porter in action.

Betts's life on campus, however, was not all tied to literature and creative writing. A freewheeling episode began with research for a term paper involving Marx and the Communist Party. To gather information, Betts wrote directly to the Soviet Embassy and to the U.S. Communist Party headquarters in New York. Quickly entered on these mailing lists, Betts began to receive "quite blatant rich propaganda—good stuff for my paper."[19] With a Stalin poster pasted on her dormitory room door, Betts went around campus in big boots. Intent on exposing communism by ridicule, Betts instead provoked gossip about her political affinities. Unknown to her, a faculty member named Lettie Rogers was defending Betts, "outraged at any intrusion into free access of information and any easy assumption that curiosity was anti-patriotic" ("Memo"). It was a useful experience and surely affected Betts, who throughout her career has sharply defended and on occasion criticized people and causes.

At the end of her sophomore year Betts had earned Phi Beta Kappa. Then in July she married Lowry M. Betts, who also belonged to the Associate Reformed Presbyterian Church. Their courtship had flourished during summer conferences at Bonclarken, the denomination's beautiful assembly grounds in Flat Rock, North Carolina. She returned to Greensboro, completed half of her junior year, and moved with her husband to his father's home in Columbia for the birth of her first child, and for Lowry Betts to complete his degree at the University of South Carolina. In June the degree (in art and philosophy) was awarded; in July the baby (LewEllyn) was born; and at the end of the summer of 1953, Doris and Lowry Betts moved to Chapel Hill. Here Lowry entered law school, and Doris Betts soon began an association with the University of North Carolina that has become legendary. That summer, too, her career as an established writer began. Her story "Mr. Shawn and Father Scott" won the *Mademoiselle* College Fiction Contest (the story appeared in the August 1953 *Mademoiselle* and later was included in *Best Short Stories of 1953*), and in November 1954 she won the first UNC-Putnam contest. The $2,000 award for *The Gentle Insurrection and Other Stories* ($1,000 as prize, $1,000 as advance on royalties) kept the young student family financially afloat for a time and transformed the would-be writer into a published author.

When her husband graduated from law school in 1956, Betts was the mother of two and now awaited the publication of her first novel, *Tall Houses in Winter*, scheduled for the fall. (It was published in 1957.) Her roles as wife, mother, and writer made life busy enough, but she was also employed full-time in Chapel Hill as office manager for Simplified Farm Record Book Company, whose logo read, "Farm Records: The story of the economic life of a Nation." Occasionally her job required overtime, as she reported to her friend and fellow writer Louise Hardeman Abbot: "[Have] done some night work this week running Varitype (I grow familiar with a thousand machines, malicious things) for the N. C. Jersey Breeders Association. We are printing their fall sales catalog."[20] Add in the typing class for the Highway Patrolmen, and it is easy enough to believe Betts when she says that *Tall Houses in Winter* was a "lunch hour" novel. Somehow Betts had also earned six semester hours at the University of North Carolina and had established valuable professional associations with Jessie Rehder (who taught creative writing and had assisted Betts with information about the UNC-Putnam prize), Phillips Russell, and C. Hugh Holman.

Russell taught a writing class, which often gathered in his home to read from their work in progress. The routine was to outfit the table with a box of saltines, a can of deviled ham, a can opener, a knife, and a bottle of rye whiskey. And then read. During one of these sessions, Russell remarked that the textile industry of North Carolina was fine subject matter for a novel, and he was puzzled that no one had taken it up. Betts decided to claim the territory, to which she had some affinity because her parents had both worked as weavers in a textile mill. Research in the textile division of nearby North Carolina State University fleshed out the historical facets of a book that Betts did write and publish, her second novel, *The Scarlet Thread*.

In the 1960s Jessie Rehder *was* the creative-writing program at the University of North Carolina. In 1966 she invited Betts to sit in on her honors writing course, which met one afternoon a week for three hours. Betts drove the 40-odd miles from Sanford, where the family had moved when Lowry Betts joined the law firm of Pittman and Staton. Plagued with heart problems, Rehder died quite suddenly at the end of the semester. On that day, Rehder had finished grading a stack of student papers. Max Steele, a friend and colleague, remembers being told that her Bible lay open at the Book of John, and that her last words were "I don't want to die." To help staff the program, the English Department offered Betts a part-time position. By this turn of bad and good fortune, Betts's teaching career—now in its third decade—at the University of North Carolina had begun.

In an article in the mid-1980s, Betts had declared that all good education must have education of character as its end. Ten years later a reporter asked if she still embraced that view. She did indeed and took the opportunity to elaborate. Part of education, she said, "is meditating on how to get along with people, or why work is not just something you do to make money but can be very satisfying in its own right, and how you choose the kind of work that uses the best part of you, and whether you owe something to people who've been less fortunate. That's what I mean by character."[21] Betts rephrased the matter elsewhere: the point of education is not about making a *living* but about making a *life*.

"Grieve, I Guess."

Since 1966, when she joined the University of North Carolina English Department as a part-time lecturer, Doris Betts has been teaching freshman composition, creative writing, and literature to students—a task, she quips, that is guaranteed to keep the arteries from hardening. Her frequent speaking appearances throughout North Carolina keep her attuned to the public's perception of the university, but she is also aware that some students enter college full of hope, but poorly prepared. Although Betts refuses to place the blame for student deficiencies totally on public-school teachers, who wrestle with crowded classes, unrealistic administrative demands, and some unmannerly or uncivil students, the fact remains that many entering students have never moved beyond banal self-expression and careless writing habits.

Astonished, they learn that Betts considers "mastery of mechanics and spelling the most primitive writing requirement, the equivalent of not spitting on the floor or not going to a party with your pants unzipped." They take another deep breath when they learn that Betts will "simply return, unread, material that sends me instead of the student to the *Harbrace Handbook*."[22]

Betts argues that composition courses should be just that—composition courses—not a passing glance at writing while concentrating on literature. For Betts, "the primary textbooks are a dictionary, a thesaurus, a handbook, and at least one page of prose which each student writes every single day."[23] That daily page must then be rewritten—ideally improving because the teacher read and thoroughly commented on the page. "If we do not teach composition in this difficult and vigorous way," Betts contends, with a warning to lazy teachers, "it is because secretly we do not follow any of the three precepts: we do not write ourselves; we are not fascinated by ways of writing; and we view composition as a second-rate activity. . . . They [freshmen] hope I will have the same faith in their unexpressed ideas as in unseen angels. And I sympathize with them because I also write; would we not all prefer to be judged for the beauty we intend and not for the mess we have written?" ("Proposals," n.p.).

Even though learning "ought to be the most natural and exciting thing human beings do," the fact is that courses such as composition demand plain hard work whose reward may be years in coming.[24] Betts likes to remember Flannery O'Connor's saying that "ours is the first age in history which has asked the child what he would tolerate learning."[25] Often required courses—including freshman English—strike students as drudgery, and left to their own devices, many "would learn nothing beyond the latest video. They need required courses" (Rogoff, 5).

They may need more than that. At a loss to understand the rationale of a high school student's writing, Betts asked the young woman what criterion she used for beginning a paragraph. "You won't tell my teacher?" the young woman asked before she confessed: "I've always made a new paragraph as soon as I have used eight blue lines of notebook paper."[26] In "Your Student Writer and Mine," Betts assured public-school teachers that professors in freshman English classes were not hiding "in ambush for the first misspelled word."[27] The goal, Betts continues, is to foster intelligent thinking, which in turn produces intelligent writing. And whereas one misspelled word will not cause disaster, Betts cautions that her students must also learn that "no stupid statement improves just because the subject and verb agree" ("Student Writer," 14). With limited state funds, politicians, as well as administrators of public schools and institutions of higher learning, have to make difficult choices. Although it is true that the university admits some students who are ill prepared, the fact remains that those students must be taught long after the uproar of finger-pointing at who-failed-to-teach-what has quieted down (Rogoff, 7). For decades Betts has been getting on with that task.

During her years as director of Freshman-Sophomore English (1972–1978), Betts made demands of students, as well as of the some 80 teaching assistants she supervised. Students learned that papers were to be submitted *on time* because, Betts argues, her agent and editor expect the same from her. The Winston cigarette commercial notwithstanding,[28] Betts's students are *not* to use "like" when "as" is correct. Such grammatical points are important, Betts contends, because correctness and precision in language produce precision in thought. Young students and the TAs are well advised to heed Betts's insistence on correct grammar and spelling and to note her contempt for "holistic" grading. She marks errors and writes marginal comments because the process helps the student, and because she herself has learned from the written comments of her editors.

While she directed freshman composition, Betts sent her staff a "Bottomless Memo," a running communiqué in which she discussed general problems and encouraged TAs to contribute useful teaching ideas at "Shop Talk Lunches" and to attend professional meetings. In the "Bottomless Memo," Betts sometimes scolded. No incoherent passage in a student's paper will improve, she wrote, with nothing more than the marginal comment "awkward." Betts stressed respect for the teaching of composition. "Shakespeare," she quipped, "has survived many bad teachers; I sometimes wonder that the English language limps along at all. But Shakespeare also has many Master Teachers; the art of writing has had part-time attention from too many of us waiting to get to 'the *real* thing.' "[29]

Occasionally the "Memo" reported a light moment. Weary from fall registration and arranging the preliminary writing tests, Betts received a 10:30 P.M. phone call from a new student. Sweating over the essay that might exempt him from freshman composition, the student called to ask, "Do the similes and metaphors have to be inside a paragraph or would we take them plain?" Betts responded, "As plain as possible, honey bunch."[30]

Betts expected TAs to resolve grade protests themselves but intervened when students appealed. She reported in the "Bottomless Memo" that a student, convinced his B+ should have been an A, had appealed. When Betts "asked what he'd do if I reviewed his file and felt the grade should be lowered," the student replied, "Grieve, I guess."[31] Betts's sense of humor, along with her administrative skill and hard work, encouraged TAs and freshmen alike. William L. Andrews, a former TA and now the Joyce and Elizabeth Hall Professor of English at the University of Kansas, recently wrote to Betts: "It's been more than two decades since you directed me and lots of other inexperienced TA's in the freshman comp program at Carolina. You did an excellent job in that capacity. I remember the program as giving me a first-rate introduction to teaching as well as instilling some real esprit de corps in everyone I knew in the program."[32]

Before she taught her first creative writing course, Betts knew some assignments to avoid: hang a famous painting in the schoolroom and let the students write an essay on it; release a cat in the room so as to get a spontaneously written description. Creative writing, Betts often says, is not a hobby for weekend amusement. She deplores the doctrinaire teacher—all rules and no passion—who dictated to students the "five requirements" of a short story: "It must be brief, contain one religious reference, include sex, have an association with society, and illustrate modesty. It served her right," Betts declared, "to get a manuscript that read in full, ' "My God!" said the Duchess, "Take your hand off my knee" ' " (*ADE*, 35–36).

Students line up (often all night) hoping for a seat in Betts's creative writing class, and enrollment constraints mean that many are turned away. For those who do get in there is no guarantee that they will actually *become* writers; however, Betts insists, they will learn to write better. Even the most talented students are urged to find a "real way" to make a living. "You can't make a living as a writer," Betts reminds them, "unless you are a commercial writer or a Stephen King or James Michener."[33] If students need proof that maintaining a steady income as a writer is perilous, Betts can point to her statement from the royalty manager at Harper and Row for the period 1 January 1979 to 30 June 1979. In the Betts Collection at the Mugar Memorial Library lies an uncashed check for $0.65—Betts's royalties for that six-month period—accompanied by an insufferable explanation. "We are now able to pay economically all earnings currently due an author regardless of the amount. Accordingly, you may find a check enclosed for an amount which is less than $1.00."[34] Betts did.

In creative-writing classes, no one can teach a good idea or a writer's view of the human condition; "life itself is too busy doing both."[35] What can and should be taught, Betts contends, "is technique because in ten years they will have forgotten everything inspiring, but they will remember the technique and will be able to use the material life has given them" (Scandling, 13). With school behind them, students have a lifetime of "wide reading and deep living" that alone will "add the other dimensions, and so slowly!"[36] Technique alone produces exercises; essential truth "will get into their stories the same way it gets into their lives—the way the peach seed is inside the peach."[37] Creative-writing courses may not produce successful novelists or short-story writers (Betts's have—Randall Kenan and Tim McLaurin are two), but they should, Betts contends, "produce students who respect and cherish language, who read more deeply and with greater understanding, who may even carry the lessons of characterization and point of view into greater weekday tolerance of their fellow man" (*ADE*, 34–35).

Betts's teaching success has been recognized in many ways. In 1990 the North Carolina Writers' Network received an anonymous donation sent from a writer who wanted to honor Doris Betts for her teaching.

One summer Betts joined John Ciardi, William Stafford, and others at a
conference at the University of Denver on teaching creative writing.
Although Betts's teaching hour was 8:30 A.M., the evaluation comments
suggest that the early hour did not curtail her enthusiasm. "The
woman," one participant wrote of Betts, "is either a born teacher or
someone who has worked hard to achieve the excellence I associate with
the ART of teaching. She was . . . prepared, not dependent upon notes
because what she said was alive inside her. Her sense of humor was so
engaging because it was not contrived, but NATURAL."[38]

Her criticism can blaze, but she wants to spur inexperienced writers,
not silence them. When she judges fiction contests, Betts points out the
obvious flaws that hinder fiction writers—"perfectly natural beginner
problems . . . like having a temperature of 99 degrees—slightly off, but
not enough to signify disease!"[39] Paying tribute to Betts during a symposium in her honor, Tim McLaurin[40] related how as a 27-year-old vet-
eran, surrounded by much younger undergraduates with quite different
writing interests, he would have left the university out of boredom and
frustration had not Betts given him "such immediate criticism and
shown an interest in my writing that went far beyond that of other
teachers. She started with the basics."[41] A marginal comment in Betts's
distinctive hand announced: "Tim, I don't ever want to explain *one more
time* the difference between *its* & *it's*. You're bright; just *learn* it & pre-
vent my apoplexy" (McLaurin, 30). Randall Kenan, recipient of the
1996 Rome Fellowship in Literature from the American Academy of
Arts and Letters,[42] also values Betts's teaching, which impressed him
"not only by the content of her instruction, but also by the form, for it
extended beyond the classroom and fulfilled one of the deepest hungers
a writing student has: to see 'how it's done.' "[43]

Although Betts has a maternal pride in these students, she has no
interest in remaining "their writing teacher." Real writers, she argues,
must "outgrow the need for teacher approval . . . There comes a time
when you'll have to decide for yourself and say, 'No, I won't change it, I
know what's good.' "[44] Not all of her creative-writing students, of
course, get into print. When she meets former students, many offer
"postgraduate excuses" to explain "why they aren't writing, haven't
been writing, have nothing in print." Betts gently interrupts to ask,
"What have you been reading?" "In that area," she says, "I have never
once been disappointed" (*ADE*, 36).

In 1967 a young high school student heard Betts speak and sent her
some of his poems. Nearly 30 years later, David L. Walker, now a profes-

sor of English at Oberlin College, wrote to Betts and enclosed a copy of the letter she had written to him about those poems of his youth. "You responded with a generosity that is still quite moving to me. To this day I still remember my excitement. And your subsequent visit to my school [Durham High School, Durham, North Carolina] was equally important. So if you're wondering here at midterm about whether all the energy you're investing is worth it—well, here's some testimony that it is."[45]

Like motherhood, community service, and university commitments, teaching has taken much of Betts's time and energy, so that her own writing has far too often had to be put aside and publication delayed. But like these other endeavors, teaching has brought its own rewards. Her attention to the teaching of students and her devotion to the University of North Carolina—she often refers to it as one word, "thisgreatuniversity"—have been as unwavering as they have been costly to her career as a fiction writer. In the *Leader,* a magazine of the North Carolina Triangle, Bill Finger writes about Betts, who, he notes, has been described by friends and former students as "bawdy, deeply religious, and most often, a great person."

If "Doris Betts" never has the ring for posterity of "Eudora Welty" or "Katherine Anne Porter," the reason might be her passion for, and investment in, the students and the buildings she passes on this ten-minute walk to lunch. But this passion might be the source of the wisdom and stamina needed for the final leap to being a full-fledged novelist, in her own eyes and—who can say?—perhaps those of the larger literary world.[46]

"thisgreatuniversity"

For over three decades, Betts has not only taught at the University of North Carolina at Chapel Hill but also been, as her colleague Professor Joseph M. Flora says, "a very visible presence. There's no one who seems *quite* to manage so much."[47] In 1987, when the Katherine Kennedy Carmichael residence hall was dedicated on the campus, Betts, in the keynote address, praised Carmichael's lifelong service to the university, which extended "from the days when women bought shoes to fit the occasion and into the days when women buy shoes to fit their feet. She was a southern lady but never a southern fool, one of those *real* women who never go out of style."[48] Many would agree that the same can be said of Doris Betts.

In the 1980s a cartoon on Betts's office door showed Lucy, the smart-mouthed girl from Charles Schultz's "Peanuts," with the caption "A woman's place is in control" (Keynote Address, 6). More than a feminist message, the caption depicts Betts's life, as she has been appointed or elected to posts at the university, chaired committees through long and difficult assignments, and spoken at fund-raisers, dedications, and celebrations. Betts's efforts during the university's bicentennial campaign were so effective that the College of Arts and Sciences expressed its gratitude in writing: "A *very* special word of thanks to you for the time and energy you've devoted to helping us shape the College's message for the Campaign. *You* are our most effective weapon!"[49]

In 1981, Betts was elected chair of the faculty (the first woman to hold that post), a three-year term filled with academic matters for debate and policy making, as well as recommendations to the chancellor.[50] (The chair also faced the annual task of encouraging participation in the faculty procession at spring commencement. In 1985, Betts's final year as chair, instead of a matter-of-duty memorandum, Betts sent to members of the general faculty a poem—"The Lame Duck's Swan Song [Sorry, Longfellow]"—which reportedly brought the faculty out.)[51] As chair, Betts pressed for greater quality of instruction, supported higher salaries for the library staff, emphasized the concerns of minority and women faculty and students, championed a grievance procedure for teaching assistants and a better advising system for students, and worked to improve faculty morale and the intellectual life of the campus. The 9 April 1985 Resolution in Appreciation of Doris W. Betts expressed "our great appreciation and love to one who surely must be the most personable and subtly effective Chairman of the Faculty in the history of the University."[52]

Although she was active in campus life, Betts's role in athletic controversy seems surprising, but she boldly stepped into the debate of that eternal question: are athletic endeavors at variance with the university's purposes and standards of conduct? As chairman of the faculty, Betts appeared in 1985 before the Board of Governors' Examining Committee on Intercollegiate Athletics. University of North Carolina president William Friday reported that Betts's opening statement got everybody's attention.

> It has been said that most college sports bear the same relationship to higher education that bullfighting bears to agriculture. I am here today on behalf of the Chapel Hill faculty to keep distinguishing what is major

from what is minor at a university, to emphasize which is the large dog of learning and which is the small tail of a win-loss record. And who wags what.[53]

Her words, President Friday continued, convinced him "that Doris had no intentions of becoming the first woman of athletics!" ("Tribute," 281). Betts concluded her remarks to the board of governors by saying the general faculty doubted "that most student athletes will become professionals, and in 10 years the speed of their judgment will become more important than the speed of their feet" ("Tribute," 281).

Betts's work in 1985 prepared her for later events. University of North Carolina faculty members were disturbed because the Educational Foundation (the Rams Club) was successfully raising 35 million dollars to construct the Smith Center at a time when financial cutbacks from the state were such "that faculty members had to buy their own stamps to write letters of recommendation for students."[54] Then in 1987 University of North Carolina football coach Dick Crum resigned under pressure. The buyout of $800,000 created controversy among the faculty. Laurence Avery, secretary of the faculty, expressed the general feeling that the figure "was all out of proportion in an educational environment. It looked as if undue pressure had been placed on the University from outside influences—namely rich alumni" (Cagle and Hicks, 6). This incident prompted 230 faculty members to sign a petition calling for an investigation into intercollegiate athletics on the campus. Former chairmen of the faculty and other university officials were convened as the Ad Hoc Committee on Athletics and the University. The group elected Doris Betts as chair. The nine-member committee met for nearly two years and then submitted 9 recommendations for national reform in intercollegiate athletics and 22 recommendations for local reform.[55]

Betts's involvement in campus affairs has been extensive. "There's very little," she says, "I haven't ended up doing"; and although the "progress of academic committees is slow," she adds, "it teaches patience" (Waldorf, 25).

Recognition has come not only in committee assignments and promotions, but also in awards: the University of North Carolina Tanner Award for distinguished undergraduate teaching (1973), the Katherine Kennedy Carmichael Award for Teaching (1980), the North Carolina Award for Women from Chi Omega Sorority (1982), the University of North Carolina Alumni Award for distinguished teaching (1991). Betts's outstanding teaching was honored nationally in 1986 when she was named a Celebrated Teacher by the Association of Departments of English. Betts joined Carolyn Heilbrun and Hazard Adams in a forum, "Celebrated Teachers, Celebrated Texts," at the 1986 Modern Language Association meeting in New York. And in 1987 the University of North Carolina Department of English created the Doris Betts Award to be given annually to a graduate student in recognition of excellence in teaching in the freshman writing program.

Betts has three times won the Sir Walter Raleigh Award for the best book of fiction that year by a North Carolinian (1958, 1965, 1973), the North Carolina Award for Literature (presented by the legislature in 1975), and the R. Hunt Parker Award from the North Carolina Literary and Historical Association (1989). In 1992 the North Carolina Humanities Council named Betts the recipient of the John Tyler Caldwell Award for the Humanities, whose citation noted her "contribution to the literary life of the nation, expressed in material that was definitely southern in subject but universal in appeal." In 1990, when Betts was awarded an honorary degree from the University of North Carolina at Greensboro (formerly Woman's College), the citation epitomized her professional life: "Deep understanding of North Carolina people, a keen eye for human foibles and a sense of the heart's ways mark all your tales, showing the writer and teacher to be one."

Although Betts's reputation in the South is strong (in 1995 *Souls Raised from the Dead* won the Southern Book Award given by the Southern Book Critics Circle), national recognition has been somewhat slower in coming. As Lee Smith said on a review-blurb of *Heading West,* "Doris Betts, who is not yet a household word, should be." That wider audience is growing. In 1973 the *New York Times* named *Beasts of the Southern Wild* one of the 20 best books of the year, and in 1974 this collection was nominated for the National Book Award. Betts's popular short story "The Ugliest Pilgrim" was adapted for film and as *Violet* won the 1981 Academy Award for the best short feature and the Special Grand Jury Award from the Houston Film Festival. In 1997 *Violet,* a musical based on "The Ugliest Pilgrim," had a successful seven-week run at Playwrights Horizons in New York. The *New York Times* included *Souls Raised from the Dead* among the best books of 1994. Betts titles have been published in England, South Africa, Italy, Holland, and Canada.

Early in the 1970s, Dr. Howard Gotlieb, director of Special Collections of the Mugar Memorial Library at Boston University, sought out and attained the papers of Doris Betts. Rather than the library of the University of North Carolina at Chapel Hill or at Greensboro, where

Betts has such close ties, Boston University acquired the papers instead. In 1972 James H. Thompson, then director of the library at the University of North Carolina at Greensboro, wrote to Betts that however glad he was her papers were well cared for in the Mugar Memorial Library, he deeply regretted that they weren't where they should be—in Greensboro, along with those of Randall Jarrell.[56]

The most rewarding recognition thus far for Betts came in 1989 when the American Academy and Institute of Arts and Letters voted her the Award of Merit for the Short Story. Irving Howe, chairman of the Award Committee for Literature that year, sent Betts the news. Betts's reply began, "What a blessed surprise." The academy's citation was singularly apt: "Doris Betts's idiosyncratic work, the subtlest modernist practice deeply colored by an intimate knowledge of and joy in her region, astonishes with its wit, passion, and sharp particularity." With this major award, Betts was clearly on the national scene.

Response at home to the Award of Merit was swift, and one letter written on University of North Carolina Basketball Office stationery brought congratulations from the legendary coach Dean Smith. (Betts almost gives Coach Smith a cameo appearance in *Souls Raised from the Dead*. When Miss Lila Torrido has lunch at the Carolina Inn, she hoped Dean Smith would be in the dining room, but as "she swept her eye over the tables, the coach was not there.")[57]

A Recovering Calvinist

In 1991 Betts was asked to be part of a presentation—"Showcasing the Faculty"—before the Board of Visitors of the University of North Carolina. The notation on her appointment book for Friday, 13 September 1991, at 4:00 P.M. reads: "Bd. of Visitors. Talk about what you do and how you do it."[58] Had she discussed all her roles, the board would have listened for a long time. When she considers her busy life, Betts often quips that the three great inventions of the twentieth century are the dishwasher, the pill, and interlibrary loans.

She balances the demands of her public life by a quiet home life with her husband of 45 years and separates home from work. While raising their three children in Sanford, North Carolina, Betts commuted to the University of North Carolina to teach. Once their children moved away from home, Doris and Lowry Betts bought an 80-acre farm near Pittsboro, in Chatham County, near Chapel Hill. Their joint responsibility in raising children was replaced by caring for the Arabian horses on the farm (named Araby for these horses and after James Joyce's short story "Araby"), some 19 of whom compete with dogs and assorted cats as pets. On the farm Betts has planted old-fashioned rosebushes, many imported from Europe, and acquired yellow-banded Italian bees to produce honey and to cross-pollinate the fruit trees.

When they are not working (her husband has retired as district judge of Chatham and Orange Counties), Doris and Lowry Betts are at home, entertaining infrequently and socializing sparingly. Their careers have been kept separate—they seldom go to hear each other give speeches. Their temperaments are nearly opposite but, happily, complementary. Her husband's parents had a conventional marriage: his father worked and his mother did "home economics," and Betts knows that deep in his heart, her husband wishes she had followed his mother's pattern (Powell, 29). Instead, Betts has pursued a many-faceted career and knows well that women can't be everything. "Juggling times, learning you couldn't be a superb cook and have just-so home entertaining, these were necessary adjustments" for Betts, whose husband, she has said, "wouldn't do household tasks even if the President were coming to dinner."[59] Still, as Betts has watched many of her married friends divorce (and one of her own children as well), her marriage has remained solidly intact. She and her husband have, she said to an interviewer, "accommodated" (Powell, 29).

Although she readily praises the advantages Chapel Hill offers as a place to live, Betts likes to get away from its atmosphere. "They're not the sort of people I grew up with or know best or write about. I find more interesting the people who do not have as many layers between them and candor, people who live life closer to the bone" (Alderson, 38). Life in Pittsboro suits her well.[60] When construction began for a planned community near Pittsboro, replete with golf course, gate house, and security guard, Betts returned home from errands and reported, "You should hear what they're saying about *that* at the feed store" (Alderson, 38). Unlike city people who want to know what your profession is and what firm employs you, people in Pittsboro "don't care that much what you do—they *assume* everybody has to work" (Alderson, 38). "You can't have it all—writer, teacher and perfect mom," she says, "but I'm not dissatisfied with any of my compromises. You might just say my life has been crowded" (Farrington, 2B).

As a writer, Betts finds her closest affinity with Walker Percy and Flannery O'Connor, and occasionally reviewers and critics link these three, whose fiction rests upon a religious foundation. In speeches, as well as in fiction, Betts often alludes to O'Connor; however, differences between the two writers' religious stance are sharp. O'Connor brings her central characters into a confrontation with grace, sometimes at the moment of death. For example, when the little boy (Harry/Bevel) in "The River" walks out into the water alone after his baptism, O'Connor "sees that moment of passing out of this life into the next as the achievement, the promotion" (W. Brown, 101). Betts, on the other hand, would prefer "to pull that boy out of the river and go give him a haircut and something to eat and leave the rest to the Father. Maybe that's a difference between Catholicism and Protestantism" (W. Brown, 101). Although Betts readily acknowledges that she is a writer who is a Christian, she stiffens to hear herself described as "a Christian writer," distrusting the word as an adjective. "I don't know about you, but if someone advertises himself as a Christian car dealer, I zip up my purse."[61] Impatient with the television evangelists and those vague feel-good believers, Betts winces when *Souls Raised from the Dead* is described as a "Christian novel." Even when merely implied, she argues, the adjective "has grown rancid from ill use," and she points to the sign displayed by a gas station located between Pittsboro and a neighboring town: WE TITHE. BUY GAS FOR JESUS. Even running on empty, Betts drives on by.[62]

Betts recently commented that as a writer she is interested in religious questions even though "religion is embarrassing to people. . . . We've flipped from the Victorian: now we can talk about sex, but death and religion are embarrassing."[63] Betts does not find religion an embarrassment and links it to writing as securely as she links it to life. Religious connections are natural whether Betts is among her fellow church members in Pittsboro or writing to publishing folk in New York.

When *Souls Raised from the Dead* came out in paperback, Rachel Rader and Kate Larkin at Simon and Schuster sent Betts flowers, which arrived as Betts and her mother returned from attending a relative's funeral. "The kinswoman we buried," Betts wrote the New Yorkers, "had won every ribbon at the local and state fairs that was available for years, had hundreds in her trunks. She could drop a pecan in a hole, stomp on it, and have a tree in a couple of years. So her love of flowers was echoed in the beautiful ones you sent—thank you again. I have admired them through today and will, tomorrow, put them on the altar at Pittsboro Presbyterian Church to remember her, so you will be obliquely in this small town at Sunday worship."[64] Frequent requests for Betts to speak come by mail and by telephone; many are from churches. In April 1987 she delivered a series of four lectures at the Durham Presbyterian

Church, preached at the 11:00 Sunday service ("Private, Public, and
Corporate Prayer" was the topic), and concluded the visit with a seminar
for ministers of the presbytery on "Telling the Story: Narrative Approaches
to Preaching."

In 1993, when she delivered the installation sermon for the Reverend
William Brettman at St. Stephen's Episcopal Church in Goldsboro,
North Carolina, Betts told of her youthful years when T. S. Eliot's lines
about churchgoing—"They do it every Sunday / They'll be all right on
Monday / It's just a little habit they've acquired"—seemed wonderfully
clever. That was probably an understandable attitude for one who at 14
had formally called upon her minister to say earnestly, "Sir, I just don't
feel sinful." Everlastingly to the man's credit, Betts said, "he neither
laughed nor cried; I know now it wouldn't have helped to analyze my
hubris; nor could he force me then to see into the future where so many
failures waited in ambush for me to choose them."[65] This Pharisee journey continued until Betts called herself "the only French existentialist
housewife in Sanford, North Carolina" (Sermon, n.p.). Her return to the
church is a long and private story, but in 1979 Betts resumed an active
religious life. She teaches Sunday school, has served as clerk of the session, and is an elder and a part-time church organist. When her neighbor Elizabeth Cooper Faircloth died, Betts delivered the graveside
remarks on 13 November 1994. Theology is integral in Betts's teaching, and when a student, puzzled by a Flannery O'Connor story, asked,
"Mrs. Betts, just what *is* 'grace'?" Betts could give a swift and precise
answer.[66]

In October 1982, three University of North Carolina campus organizations sponsored Billy Graham in a weeklong lecture series. Attendance,
the newspaper reported, exceeded 30,000. With several other faculty
members, Betts addressed the audience during Graham's visit. Her
remarks, "Faith and Intellect," began: "I belong to the tribe of the Apostle Thomas—a natural doubter, always wishing I could have touched the
wound myself, could have done the definitive study to prove the Shroud
of Turin."[67]In citing a catalog of "allergies" that create doubt, Betts anticipated the theme of *Souls Raised from the Dead*. "Some of you have found
faith as easy and natural as breathing in and out. Some of us are like people with allergies: physics can ruin us for awhile; biological determinism
will give us a bad weekend; Oral Roberts embarrasses us; and we have a
chronic case, like Ivan Karamazov, of despairing over evil, undeserved
pain and the suffering of the world's children" ("Faith," ts.). Echoing
eighteenth-century American theologian Jonathan Edwards's famous

image, Betts reminded her sophisticated academic audience that the intellect is, after all, not everything. "And to us, too, sometimes when we are hanging by a slender thread over the chasm of what we cannot solve and do not understand, to us in our helplessness the Good News of God's love in Christ comes down and speaks to the strongest, most intricate, most prideful intellect" ("Faith," ts.).

Such open avowal of Christian principles contradicts the general atmosphere of a major state university where church participation is relegated to one's private life, a view Yale law professor Stephen Carter explores in *The Culture of Disbelief: How American Law and Politics Trivialize Religious Devotion,* a book Betts admires. "The message of contemporary culture," Carter suggests, says "that it's perfectly all right to believe that stuff . . . but you really ought to keep it to yourself."[68] Betts does not keep it to herself, and it is impossible to look closely at her fiction without taking into account her religious concerns. From Susan Ketchin's book *The Christ-Haunted Landscape: Faith and Doubt in Southern Fiction,* Betts has borrowed a phrase to describe herself—"a recovering Calvinist."

Several years ago, Betts spoke at a University of Alabama symposium on writers and style, tracing the roots of her own writing style to her Associate Reformed Presbyterian upbringing. Glancing at symposium colleagues, Betts saw that references to the Westminster Catechism and Scripture puzzled nonsouthern panelists such as William Gass and Donald Barthelme. Later Betts sent a copy of her remarks to Walker Percy, who replied like a kindred spirit: "A hundred years from now southern writers will still be carrying on in this biblical idiom, totally baffling the western world" (*Bookmark,* 3–4).

Betts sees that biblical narrative bends everything to a purpose, and even though some of these narratives do not furnish didactic teaching and others may convey a moral that seems ambiguous at best, "all these stories have theme and purpose" (*Bookmark,* 9). Southern writers share this mind-set, Betts argues, and "like their books to have a point" (*Bookmark,* 9). Unlike Flannery O'Connor, Betts does not draw large and startling pictures for the nearly blind or shout to the almost deaf to get their attention; her characters do not experience dramatic confrontations with the moment of grace. Instead, her characters are rather like "the descendants of Job's second cousins once removed"; they struggle through the mundane, if perilous, ups and downs of their lives "until in the end God does not so much answer their questions as silence them, simply by being there, so that my characters end by saying—or maybe whispering—'Mine eye seeth Thee.' Some of them might add, 'That *is* You, isn't it?' " ("Whispering Hope," 80).

In "Faith and the Unanswerable Questions: The Fiction of Doris Betts," the late David Holman argues that "the ability to confront doubts, to acknowledge them and find a faith within that acknowledgment is the first and necessary step to becoming fully human."[69] And if fictional characters are to go through this process, they do so because the religious faith of the author is real. Many writers use biblical images as simply a part of a shared tradition, but Reynolds Price likes to add that he and Betts *believe* all this.[70]

"I Never Stand in Line"

In 1979 professor Mary Anne Ferguson suggested in a conference paper, "Southern Writers: Beyond the Tradition. The Case of Doris Betts," that if a writer of even Welty's stature is perceived as "minor," "how can younger Southern women writers escape such categorization?"[71] For Betts to avoid being considered minor, Ferguson contends, she must "produce fiction which recreates a traditional mode; she must produce a sizable oeuvre"—in other words, novels (rather than short stories) that will compare favorably with the work of men (Ferguson, 7). Ferguson argues that Betts "has the talent and the experience; the question is whether she has the will to commit herself more fully" (Ferguson, 7). She concludes her paper by calling Betts "one of those women achievers who deny that they are feminists," and by suggesting that if Betts "sought more militantly a room of her own and five hundred pounds, she would gain the sense of her own value needed to sustain great work" (Ferguson, 8).

Since the mid-1970s, Betts has concentrated on writing novels with growing success. At the same time, she has maintained her academic and public commitments. Furthermore, she is a feminist, *not* just a woman achiever; she has been sympathetic to the women's movement but critical of certain aspects.

In 1954, when the phrase "women's movement" was hardly a glint in any female eye, Betts wrote her friend Louise Hardeman Abbot that marriage does *not* automatically stop a woman's individuality so long as the husband realizes his wife is a human being, not a broom. After all, Betts quipped, "you can buy a broom for $1.49 anyway."[72] Although Betts maintains traditional roles—wife, mother, and now grandmother—she knows that housework can stifle a woman's writing life.

Pondering the story when Mary is praised for staying in the presence of Christ and her sister Martha chided for continuing with the daily tasks, Betts sympathizes with Martha. She can hear Martha shouting from the cookstove in the kitchen, "Well, goddamit, somebody has to do it! You think this is how I meant to spend my life?"[73]

Betts's stationery reflects the pattern of her life. Centered at the top is Alumni Distinguished Professor of English; on the left side, her campus address down through the fax number; to the right, her other self—Mrs. L. M. Betts, 795-B Goldston Road, Pittsboro, NC 27312. Marriage has not turned Betts into a broom, even though hers began in a sacrificing way familiar to so many women in post–World War II America. Betts quit school and became a secretary to help support her husband through law school. "By the time he graduated we already had two children, so there wasn't a chance for me to finish my education."[74]

Nevertheless, Betts's career at the University of North Carolina has produced a list of firsts. Without the A.B. degree, Betts was named the first full professor in the Department of English (the chairman said to her quietly, "You did finish high school, didn't you?"). She was the first woman to direct the Freshman English Program, to receive the Katherine Carmichael Teaching Award, to be named Alumni Distinguished Professor, and to be elected chair of the faculty. In March 1995, Betts joined other women honored at a reception for "First Women in Orange County," women who had broken both gender and racial barriers in Chapel Hill and its environs.

If she is neither an angry nor a militant feminist, Betts has always been sensitive to women's lives. In "My Grandfather Haunts This Farm" (1977), Betts remembers her grandmother. Long outliving her husband, weakened by age, and powerless to claim independence, old Mrs. Freeze spent her last years "in other women's houses, without ever adjusting to a single electrical appliance," ("Grandfather," 86). In the 1970s, Betts distanced herself from the more radical aspects and, at times, from even the center of the women's movement. Why, she was asked in 1975, did she not publish under her maiden name (Waugh) rather than following the less feminist course by using her husband's name and giving up her own identity? The writing world, Betts quipped, already had two prominent Waughs, Alex and Evelyn. "I am not one of those MS. people," she said. "Besides, I was tired of standing at the end of lines with the W's."[75]

In the 1970s Betts found that the women students at the University of North Carolina resembled her own classmates 20 years earlier at

Woman's College—women ready to cast aside the southern belle image and make college a springboard to a career, not the means to find a husband. Although Betts has always supported women's liberation, she is "not one who joins groups and protests."[76] Not enthralled with the consciousness-raising groups, Betts does sympathize with abused women, whose plight must be redressed, yet insists that women should not whine when they can outwit. "If you happen to work for a man who thinks you are inferior, he has betrayed himself; and if you cannot outwit him maybe you are inferior" (Riener, 7). Women ought to be independent, Betts maintains, and independence had better come from themselves: "I don't like anyone telling me how I ought to live my life," Betts said, "and I don't like it any better when Gloria Steinem does it. If you like darning socks why should you go out making sculpture? It's not a social problem. I wish society would mind its own business."[77] The women's movement was inevitable; at the same time, Betts sees the larger human picture. "It never occurred to me when I was young," she told a reporter, "that life was fair and it hasn't been. It's not fair; it's not fair to men or women. What is so amazing is that so many men and women manage in spite of that to be intelligent and kind and responsible human beings. That's what is worthwhile."[78]

A prominent figure in the university and in North Carolina, Betts is often asked how she does so many things and how she manages to keep her professional and home lives going. Although Betts knows that one never makes such inquiries of a man, she explains that she has "a lot of physical energy. That's a gift. I am compulsive. I work very hard. I don't waste energy in blame or guilt. I did when I was younger. I don't pause. I don't watch. I don't wait. . . . I never stand in line."[79]

In 1987 Betts was nominated as a candidate for the chancellorship of the University of North Carolina. Her letter to the Chancellor's Search Committee represents a culmination of her academic career. In declining the nomination, Betts never doubts "that a competent woman is capable of doing this difficult job," a woman possessed of the same "high character and special abilities" expected in top male contenders.[80] With feminist irony, Betts explains that her husband's position creates her first reason for declining. The woman candidate, Betts said, "ideally should be married to the kind of husband skilled at being a University host and full-time supporter. You will see immediately that while my husband could manage those duties, he could not do so and continue his own professional responsibilities as District Judge in Chatham and Orange Counties, which sometimes bring into his court University of North

Carolina students and / or faculty" (Search letter). Betts listed other reasons for withdrawing her name: she was 55, 5 to 10 years older than she believed "the optimum age an energetic and overworked Chancellor should be," and her desire to write books overshadowed her administrative ambition (Search letter).

Feminist in Fiction

Betts's fiction explores many issues that interest feminists. For example, in her most popular short story, "The Ugliest Pilgrim," Betts creates Violet Karl, who believes the way to happiness is a beautiful face and body—the message of modern advertising—and who must learn that beauty is, after all, only skin deep. In "The Story of E," an uncollected short story, Betts writes of a rape where the victim fights back and survives. Some readers felt that in letting the victim get on with her life, Betts minimized the seriousness of the attack. Betts disagrees. She gave careful consideration to a *major* trauma, but Betts will not concede that claiming victimization always works. It is unfortunate, Betts says, "that part of the women's movement slid in that direction. It's understandable. And there's real victimization. I don't mean to minimize that. But whining is simply not a useful response. And it's not a pragmatic response."[81]

Betts sympathizes when women are denied those things that define them as a person. In her 1997 novel *The Sharp Teeth of Love,* Betts lingers over the memory of the Donner party as they make their way west, miscalculating the difficulty and encountering unexpected dangers, especially from the weather. Betts describes her reaction as *feminist* when she thinks of the deprivations Tamsen Donner suffers on the journey.[82] Finding Tamsen's possessions unnecessary for the survival of the party, the men insisted that her wildflower collection, her watercolors, her journals, and her books (packed and taken in the hope of continuing her school teaching) be jettisoned. With that loss she loses much of her*self.*

In an early story, "Necromancer" (1970), Betts gives a passing glance to Hawthorne's "Dr. Heidegger's Experiment" as a group of old people gather and try to outwit time. A flashback of 65 years tells of a mismatched pair: a then young Mr. Morgan braces up to tell his mama that he intends to marry Christobel Gaines. At this news, "Mama Morgan wanted to faint, but the waxed floor was too hard."[83] After she rallies with the help of smelling salts, Mama Morgan announces, "You'll not live here!" and when Christobel asks, " 'How come?' Mama Morgan grew faint again" ("Necromancer," 144). But the old lady has her way in the end, taming Christobel and molding her into the "lady" Mama Morgan will have as a daughter-in-law. During the first year of the marriage, the house is kept shuttered as they remake Christobel—"laced her up and bound her up and shut her up." As the training succeeds, "guests were admitted, Christy was allowed to sit in the parlor with her eyes down, reciting first-grade stuff ('Yes, indeed,') and then third-grade and sixth ('Miz Martin, your little boy is the sweetest thing. Do you take sugar?'). At last she could pour tea without scalding anybody and glide around in her long dress as if she had nothing below the waist but one oiled wheel" ("Necromancer," 144). The spunky girl is transformed into the proper, but empty, lady. In 1970 Betts's feminist message was there for the reading.

In a passage not included in the published version of her essay "Daughters, Southerners, and Daisy," Betts reflects on the freedom women writers enjoy today. "Whether shy or garrulous, today's woman writer might well run for mayor like Norman Mailer or of her own free will practice her craft in privacy like May Sarton, live with her mother like Marianne Moore, or mix art with teaching and anti-war activism like Grace Paley. Nowadays she can embrace or resist [being a] celebrity; go out and live, or stay home and create; most women writers do both."[84] Not only do women writers now have this greater freedom, but also they profit from the time-honored tradition of women's friendships, what Mary Gordon has called the company of women. In the early years of both their married lives, Betts said to her friend Louise Hardeman Abbot, "do write—your letters accomplish the old hymnal adage and throw out lifelines not in storms but in the worse situation of quiet seas and cloudless skies and generally dull circumstances."[85] Betts thinks friendship is important for women writers, most of whom learn, as did Betts, that becoming a writer is more than saying she must simply work harder, "be a superwoman."[86] Communication with fellow women writers helps, and it is, Betts says, "a great relief to be able to say, 'Listen, kid, you're going to be tired, and as soon as you've gotten to the best sentence you've ever written, the baby will cry or vomit' " (Howard, 43). Such shared experiences, Betts argues, make women candid about the difficulty of balancing the nursery and the kitchen against the writing desk and encourage women to support each other. In the mid-1990s, Betts says, "certainly the liveliest writing in North Carolina is by women, and they're nearly all good friends" (Howard, 43). (Another network that Betts has encouraged is the local assistance available from the Women's Center at University of North Carolina, where since 1979 the center has extended "friendship to women in the community" through programs and seminars "on everything from budgeting to outliving teenage children.")[87]

In her introduction to *Southern Women Writers: The New Generation,* Betts rejects the Whitman-Dickinson contrast that says that women writers, unlike men, mirror the daily restrictions of their lives, are inadequately directed outward, lack social consciousness, and conclude their stories "with such tiny private victories or self-esteem for their heroines that plots diminish to trivial pursuits."[88] Betts argues that these southern women writers are fully aware of themselves and of their subject matter. They consider their imagined houses of fiction "more as daily manifestations of reality than as refuges from reality" and understand Eleanor Ross Taylor's advice: "Stay here where the suffering's homemade, sure to fit" (Introduction, 7).

When Betts won a Guggenheim Fellowship in 1958, her creative-writing teacher, Phillips Russell, hoped that the prize would give her some leisure time. Russell was sure that even with her considerable energy, Betts could not continue to keep up a house, look after her children and husband, review books, write another novel, maintain some social life, and answer the telephone. But Betts did all that—and more.

Staring at Reporters—Betts as Journalist

Long before reporters became television icons, they fascinated Betts, and she declared in a 1957 newspaper column that she had never "outgrown staring at reporters . . . they always (especially out of town) look so important and self-contained, tote their own typewriters, rake the crowd with shrewd glances, . . . are the only ones to defy the No-Smoking regulations. . . . [They] led us toward a journalistic career in the first place."[89] The lure of reporting has made Betts a consistent contributor to newspapers throughout North Carolina as columnist and occasional feature writer. For a good part of 1957, in addition to writing a daily column for the *Sanford Daily Herald,* Betts also proofread the entire newspaper, made up the social page, edited it, and wrote the heads. "I like it," she said, "and am gradually learning to do a passable job, having first made all the errors of ignorance."[90]

Her lifelong newspaper life began during her senior year in high school. On Saturday, 22 October 1949, "Hitting the High Spots" first appeared in the *Statesville Daily Record.* Finding the task more daunting than she expected, Betts began her second column (which appeared five days later) with strong reservations. "With six headaches, three packs of typing paper, and one column to my credit, it has occurred to me that there must be an easier way to make a living. I am considering basket-weaving as a profession."[91]

She persevered, however, and her column appeared weekly, though not always on the same day of the week, through June commencement.[92] At this time the population of Statesville was 21,375, and the paper's press run was 5,150. Next to local editorials and accounts of weddings and church meetings, the paper ran Drew Pearson's syndicated column, "Washington Merry-Go-Round." It was a time when a person could walk into the Princess Cafe and get Thanksgiving dinner for 95¢.

For the most part, Betts's column contained predictable high school preoccupations—club and sports activities, special school events (book week, charity drives), accounts of drama productions, and gossip. The column reflected a seemingly innocent time, an era when the most worrisome school problem was how to encourage student drivers to exit the parking lot in an orderly fashion. Concealed weapons in book packs, metal detectors at school entrances, and drug sales behind the stairs were troubles in the future. Although the content was often trivial, Betts occasionally confronted substantive issues, moving beyond school news and gossip to champion the cause for a larger recreation center in Statesville.

Betts argued that Valdese, a much smaller town, enjoyed a bigger facility and a wider range of programs. "Why," she asked in her column, "can't Statesville also build a larger center to accommodate the leisure hours of her citizens?" (27 October 1949: 4). When the Lexington, North Carolina, sportswriter Scoop McCrary complained about Statesville's numerous sports championships, Betts called him "unjust, narrow-minded, and a very poor reporter" (8 March 1950: 7). As it turned out, McCrary was calling for changes in the size of the conference and telephoned Betts—armed with facts and statistics—to tell her so. Left without a case, Betts wrote "an apology to a very nice man in Lexington who is patient with high school girls when they act like grammar-graders" (14 March 1950: 7).

When the new physical education building for the high school was completed, Betts jumped into the fray because the city of Statesville wanted to control the building and the scheduled sports events. This time she had her facts. The building *was* available for outside tournaments, and local students assisted with these special games. Use was not exclusively for the high school's events. Confident, Betts reminded her readers that the building, after all, was built for the physical education programs of the students and for the city to complain now was absurd. "If the city wanted the present gym," she argued, "why not put in a bid for it before, instead of waiting until it was all finished and then hollering like mad?" (31 March 1950: 5). This issue caused quite a stir. The members of the Jaycees "have buzzed about my head like angry hornets," she reported, and her boss, editor Jay Huskins, opposed her position (31 March 1950: 3). Nevertheless, Betts felt her position was right and represented the majority of the student body.

During her senior year, Betts was the only girl covering high school sports, and she braved the men's sports world by entering the press box during a football game. "As the game progressed, each grew more annoyed at the fact that a mere (whisper the word) girl! woman! Female! was keeping up with the score fairly well." Then Betts flashed the score sheets for the *Greensboro Daily News* (20 January 1950: 3). All Betts did was call in the score to the *News,* but the men in the press box thought—at least momentarily—that she represented the larger city newspaper, and she let that impression linger without a word.[93] The early thrill of leaning into the ticket window and murmuring, "Press," never left her.

Her part-time work on the local paper brought several advantages: she learned to play poker, a fellow sportswriter in Greensboro helped her secure a student job with the Woman's College news bureau (making college expenses possible), and 40-odd years later she was named a member of the *Statesville Daily Record*'s Old-Timers Club.

When she moved to Sanford, Betts wrote special-feature articles for the *Sanford Daily Herald,* and during 1957 and 1958, she published a daily column called "Ladies First." She used the pretentious editorial "we" throughout these columns (others on the paper staff followed the same practice), which apprised readers of concerts, golden wedding anniversaries, theater productions in nearby Pinehurst, projects of local organizations, church activities, and local sports events. Frequently Betts mentioned new books by North Carolina writers, reported on events in nearby Chapel Hill, and occasionally took up political and social issues.

In several columns Betts met the integration issue, if not head-on, at least with a more open mind than much of the South exercised at that time. Appalled by the ranting in *The Citizens' Council,* a small newspaper published in Jackson, Mississippi, and edited by W. J. Simmons, Betts argued that the "American way . . . grants us diversity of opinion all the way from the near-socialist to the Citizens Councils, and imposes the restriction only that we shall not do each other (that is society) harm by our beliefs and our expressions of them."[94] The Civil Rights Act did not pass Congress until 1964; Betts's stance in 1957 was liberal.

Throughout her career, Betts has published occasional feature articles in various newspapers, particularly the *Charlotte Observer,* the *Greensboro Daily News,* and the *Raleigh News and Observer.* In 1994 she joined some dozen Chapel Hill area citizens (including former university president William Friday and Algonquin Press editor Louis Rubin) as a contributor to the "Village Voice" column in the *Chapel Hill News.* The topics ranged from local to international politics, from race relations to personal experiences. Betts (who contributed one column a month) generally began with a personal experience, always producing an engaging, often amusing, and always informative narrative. (Had Betts ever chosen to concentrate her writing exclusively as a newspaper columnist, she might well have been an Ellen Goodman or an Erma Bombeck.)

Most prominent in Betts's career as journalist are two articles in *Life*—in 1980, a piece on first lady Rosalynn Carter, "The First 'Good Ole Girl,' "[95] and in 1981, an article on the infamous case of Atlanta's missing and murdered children.[96]

Betts visited the White House on 17 and 18 January 1980, spending an hour with Mrs. Carter, whom Betts found "admirable, but not very exciting. . . . She has a polite smile and laugh, but she has no sense of irony."[97] In 1981 *Life* magazine wanted an article on Atlanta's murdered and missing children written from a southern woman's point of view and asked Betts to take on the assignment. From her interviews in Atlanta, Betts was most impressed with the dignity the victims' mothers maintained in the face of tragedy. Editors at *Life* tinkered with Betts's article up to the time of publication as new information filtered in from the Atlanta investigation. Reaction from *Life* editors was positive; the text editor, Campbell Geeslin, called Betts "an absolutely wonderful writer" and said her piece was "the best thing we've seen on the subject."[98]

Newspaper writing provided a link with the fiction that Betts was always working on. She was grateful to James A. Chaney, a newspaper man, who in the 1950s published "any number of Sunday features from me, some of them rather poor (I know now) and often for as much as $75, which was high butter-and-egg-money at the time! . . . The features helped generate a Tar Heel audience for the fiction I was also struggling to learn to write."[99]

Chapter Two

One Woman's Intriguing Mind:
A Life of Writing and
the Story Collections

The Writing Habit

If you're going to write, Betts told a reporter in 1975, you'd better be hard on yourself. "Nobody licenses you. NOBODY pays you a salary."[1] And Betts might well have added: Nobody makes the time available—especially for women. When her own three children were young, Betts juggled their needs with whatever writing was at hand. Asked to describe her "ideal writing day," she replies that she has never had one. Schedules get disrupted, and even an hour saved for writing may end up a 10-minute session instead. Still, if she were to have that ideal day, "it would begin with everybody waiting on me instead of the other way around. I don't believe there's a woman around who wouldn't say that."[2]

Interruptions do occur—a class must be taught, papers graded, a sick child tended to—but Betts insists that writers, particularly women writers, "can't blame the world. It's something you do to yourself. Life just simply admits of many interruptions" (Powell, 22). Some women resent the lack of sustained time; some, of course, are stunned into silence by interruptions. Betts just goes to the stove, turns the bacon, sits down, and writes another sentence. Because family and professional opportunities compete for her attention, Betts says, "there are tradeoffs, it seems to me, constantly. I wouldn't have had it any other way" (Powell, 30). Nevertheless, the trade-offs have enriched Betts's life at a price. When *Souls Raised from the Dead* appeared in 1994, she had not published a book in well over a decade because her "nonwriting" workday is 16 hours. Writing is extra, and she has "no patience with people who tell me they would write fiction if they only had the time."[3]

In the 1950s many women settled for domestic bliss and did not pursue careers; Betts wanted more. By 1954 she was expecting her second child but still writing. "Don't let them fool you," she wrote Louise

Hardeman Abbot, "about being married and writing . . . the old business that being married is like being dead anyway, in terms of any individuality."[4] A married woman *could* avoid becoming "a breathing laun-
dromat, cook, dishwasher, diaper-changer, sewing machine, and
vacuum." And Betts believes that "married life is the BEST way to grow
in whichever directions you choose, writing being one" (Abbot, letter, 10
September 1954). Marriage did not stifle Betts's writing. Between February and August 1954, she completed "another book's worth of short
stories, some 86,000 words, in addition to the work on the novel. That
makes between 150,000 and 200,000 words I've done in six months,
which strikes me as a high rate of output and pleases me very much."[5]

While women try to write, Betts knows that "nobody fries their eggs
and irons their clothes."[6] Furthermore, Betts believes that women more
than men have a natural tendency to solve problems if they can, adjust
and compromise if they can't. Most women can't "pick up and just leave
their problems behind" but must "stay at home and feed that baby, tend
that old woman, wash that dead body" (Ketchin, 253).

Close family ties may also make women more reluctant than men to
tell all. They may avoid delicate subject matter and controversial themes
to spare the sensibilities of maiden aunts and second cousins and living
parents. Such hesitation is not limited to southern women writers, as
Mary Gordon can attest. At a family funeral, Gordon listened to a relative's attack: "I just want to tell you I can't stand your books. None of
us can." Then a cousin, a nun, grasping Gordon's hand, had her say. "I
just feel I need to tell you that I think your books are dreadful."[7] If you
kill off a person in a novel, Betts has remarked, none of your neighbors
really think you yourself have homicidal tendencies; when they read sex
scenes that you've written, they look at your "husband sympathetically
at the A & P."[8] Yet if a woman writer ends her novel with a happy marriage—as Betts does in *Heading West* and in *The Sharp Teeth of Love*—
some reviewer is sure to call it mere women's fiction.

Male or female, Betts insists that "no writer suffers from constant
work and thought and revision," provided the revision process helps
rather than stifles.[9] Good editing, Betts says, is invisible—"only its
absence shows."[10] And although editors often help writers, their suggestions are not always correct, as Betts knows from experience.

After Putnam's published Betts's first two books *(The Gentle Insurrection and Other Stories* and *Tall Houses in Winter)*, Walter Mitten became
her editor and sent Betts "things to read that made it very clear that he
thought I ought to be writing pop fiction."[11] Indeed, Putnam's had

wanted Betts to turn *Tall Houses in Winter* into "a sort of 'problem' novel about a nice middle-aged old man with homespun philosophical ideas who has cancer, and who finds meaning in life through his nephew. Appropriate tears here and yonder. Liberal use of a God of the Norman Vincent Peale Variety—How to have peace of mind tho afflicted with cancer. To all of this I have said a polite no-thank-you, that is not my novel, even if it costs us the $500 which we will need."[12] At age 22, Betts stood by the way she felt her fiction should be written.

Happily Betts found a more congenial editorial home, publishing her next four books at Harper and Row, where M. S. "Buzz" Wyeth was her editor. That amiable association, however, ended. Even though Betts made substantive revisions of her seventh book, Wyeth still was not satisfied and declined to publish what was at that time called *Stepping Westward*. Betts later secured a contract with Knopf, where editorial advice pressed for changes she resisted. "I wasn't about to change the end. . . . it was exactly as it should have been. I waited a year and made some other changes on my own and eventually they bought the manuscript."[13] Betts finds her current editor, Ann Close, congenial and supportive.

One of her earliest accomplishments at the University of North Carolina was *Creative Writing: The Short Story,* the manual for English c34F, offered through the extension program. On page 3, students met Betts's pragmatic approach: "We all learn to write by writing, not by intending to do so." Throughout her career, Betts has written about ordinary people—yeoman farmers, weavers in textile mills, sawmill workers, filling station operators, mechanics, carpenters, house painters, ward heelers, policemen, barbers, waitresses, beauty shop owners. Half-jokingly, an interviewer once asked if there were any moonshiners in her family, and Betts shot back, I'll never tell. Although many of her characters are unsophisticated and not highly educated, Betts thinks they "are as deep and profound as Ph.D's; they simply lack the vocabulary to convey their inner lives," and she sees it as "the writer's duty to put into words what it is like to be a human being in this world, even for the inarticulate" (Cook, 4A). Certainly some of Betts's most important characters struggle unsuccessfully to speak their inmost thoughts. Violet Karl ("The Ugliest Pilgrim"), for example, keeps her scriptural references and arguments written in her notebook, a safeguard in case her speech fails to convince the TV preacher to heal her face of its unsightly scar.

In Betts's fiction, ordinary people get on with their lives, often endure suffering (which deepens their lives), and a few, primarily women characters, undergo substantial change. Betts has little patience with stories that read like "dehumanized word games, linguistic ballets whose point was the dance itself—John Barth for example, some of whose stories turn in on themselves like snakes swallowing their own tails."[14] Betts clearly prefers the realistic approach of nineteenth-century fiction writers. She thinks a story "ought to have a point" and would prefer that point to be "on the right side," like the Old Testament stories (Powell, 30). One must, however, avoid being obtrusively didactic and preachy and should produce fiction that shows what you value and what you know is pure trivia.

Whether traditional or highly experimental, writers *must* get on with it. If they wait around for an ideal environment, they may, Betts contends, turn their lives "into a long period of nothing but waiting, and provide an excuse for doing nothing" (*StoryQuarterly,* 71). These last years of the twentieth century may not be conducive to creative work, but Betts knows there have been "no good ages, no good societies, only good individuals" (*StoryQuarterly,* 71). "A recovering Calvinist" *knows* that the world has always been a fallen one and that counting upon unrealistic expectations is doomed. Never denying the religious aspect in her work, Betts does not think of herself as a didactic writer or a teller of parables. Indeed, she knows "that not everybody is called to be an apostle and I don't feel so called."[15] Fiction probably does not alter "circumstances or reality," but Betts believes that it can "speak the truth to people who hear it. And that's quite sufficient" (Harmon, 52).

Briefly, on Long Subjects

Betts takes her favorite definition of the short story from Chekhov's "I can speak briefly on long subjects," finding in these words a "short-story writer's statement of vocation [that] covers both the smallness of the form and the largeness of its implications."[16] The influence of Chekhov hovers in Betts's classroom as she urges her writing students to create pictures rather than a page of useless words. To illustrate, Betts reads Chekhov's line "The man sat in the grass." That, she says, is the picture. "Students frown. To start so simply seems a betrayal of 12 years of public school English."[17] Irked by the restrictions implied by "southern writer" or "woman writer," Betts prefers the term "regional writer"— one who uses the immediate place she or he knows to comment upon much larger concerns—as did Chekhov, who "wrote the universe into Russia" (*StoryQuarterly*, 70).

Betts feels a kinship with Walker Percy and with Flannery O'Connor, although when the first comparisons to O'Connor were made, Betts "had never read a word she'd written."[18] On the whole, Betts says, "male writers have influenced me more, I think, by and large . . . just as in my personal life, I think men have influenced me a great deal more than women."[19] And for southern writers, no male writer is more influential than Faulkner. Eudora Welty once remarked that if she were assigned to write something that was influenced by Faulkner, "My pen would drop from my hand."[20] Flannery O'Connor's humorous words suggest similar respect and distance. "Nobody wants his mule and wagon stalled on the same track the Dixie Limited is roaring down."[21]

Betts, too, admires Faulkner, and in the mid-1950s, when she was working for the Simplified Farm Record Book Company in Chapel Hill, she asked the salesman covering Mississippi to send her a Faulkner souvenir. Years later, when she gathered material for the Mugar Memorial Library, Betts included the memorandum this salesman had sent her from Oxford. Betts no longer remembered the salesman's last name, identifying him as Hank E. Although Hank failed to send a souvenir, his memorandum, vivid and apparently disingenuous, deserves—after some 45 years—to be in print.

> Well, Hon, I tried, and should I run on to anything in the future about the gentleman, I shall pass it along. Faulkner is about what I expected to find, in looks, about 5 ft. 6, slight, greying, small mustache, grey, needed a shave, his clothes were messy, green sport coat and grey trousers, all of which needed a good cleaning. He was sucking on a pipe, with nothing in it. The house is large, Southern colonial, with columns out front, mostly white with some green trim. Needed lots of attention. Beautiful setting for a home, back among a large grove of oaks and pine trees, with a circular drive leading up, roadway full of holes, had to drive in low gear to stay in the car, such a road. Half dozen mongrel dogs running around. A saddle horse in the barnyard, and an old negro man, yard man I guess, working around the barn. That gives the picture pretty well, Picturesque and interesting, even tho' ill-kept.
> Love, Hank

Travel has also influenced Betts. Asked if there has been a single event in her writing life that created a turning point, Betts replies that "in a way I would say going to the Grand Canyon was a turning point in that it got me out of being so 'South-focused.' "[22] That 1971 trip and subsequent western journeys formed the core of *Heading West* and *The Sharp Teeth of Love*. "There's just something about a new *place*," Betts says, "in which your eye is sharpened for the things which you are by now walking past without paying attention within your own neighborhood. And that's why I understand people who have left the South can write about the South better because they have a different lens to look at it" (Evans, 4).

Fairly early in their association, Betts sent her agent, Diarmuid Russell, three stories, and Russell's brief comments immediately influenced Betts. "Break now the habit," Russell told her, "of writing your stories focused on either lunatics or children because since they create their own world, you do not have to make it justified or plausible. You have closed yourself off from criticism and that's too easy" (Evans, 6). (The publication of *Author and Agent: Eudora Welty and Diarmuid Russell,* gives further evidence of Russell's skill and judgment.)[23]

By 1973 Betts had published six books—three collections of short stories and three novels—and her most successful volume from the critics' point of view was her short-story collection *Beasts of the Southern Wild,* which Jonathan Yardley described as indisputably "fiction of the first order."[24] She had also been teaching creative writing in the short story for several years and now felt she had demonstrated the skills of that genre. In 1978 she commented to a reporter that "it's a real temptation always to do what you do well and trade on it," but she added quickly, "if you don't change, you definitely stop growing."[25] So Betts has in middle age concentrated on writing novels, because writing short stories had "become too easy" and because that genre did not allow her to include "the things that I had learned by being middle-aged and older" (Powell, 20). The novel requires greater length and time span, more complexly developed characters, more involved subplots. Since *Beasts of the Southern Wild* appeared, Betts has published individual stories, but not another collection; she has instead published three novels: *Heading West* (1981), *Souls Raised from the Dead* (1994), and *The Sharp Teeth of Love* (1997). Reviews of *Heading West* were generally quite favorable, and *Souls Raised from the Dead* enjoyed an enthusiastic reception. Nevertheless, Betts knows that the shift from successful short-story writer to successful novelist remains difficult.

Good short-story writers, as well as talented novelists tinkering with their methods, Betts says, "suspend time long enough to drive readers down the layers asking 'why' with such aroused curiosity that they forget the more primitive question of 'what happened next.' "[26] Betts thinks that Anne Tyler, by persistently "tinkering" with her writing methods, "learned also how to outwit the weaknesses most writers risk when they first switch from short story to longer novel form" ("Fiction,"

36). The writer's themes, for example, must be rich enough to with-stand the exposure of 80,000 words or more. Eccentric or overblown characters that suit the short story must inhabit the longer work with-out falling into narcissism, hyperbole, or theatricality. In the process of shifting genre, some short-story writers produce novels whose every chapter remains a ministory, a weakness that Betts says plagued Tyler's early work. If Tyler still does not take many technical risks or undertake the sweep of time and history that marks the work of major writers, she is, Betts argues, a successful novelist, having moved from the short story to produce "a distinctive, dense, Tyler-type novel, dependent on charac-ter, made resonant by memory" ("Fiction," 36). If Doris Betts has not created a "Betts-type" novel, she has not in part because she has taken many risks.

Of Love and Mortality

Betts has always been intent on producing fiction that touches the heart. Early in her career, she was identified as a southern writer who portrayed women characters struggling for independence and identity. Betts has not so much shifted from that emphasis as she has concen-trated on "fiction as subtle investigation into the human need for reli-gious faith and responsibility."[27] For over 30 years, Betts has been remarkably consistent in the views she has held, attacking in her fiction people who, "expecting the free gift of happiness, did not choose to pro-duce and share it" (*StoryQuarterly,* 70). Her most interesting characters learn that life is not a matter of finding happiness on one golden day. They learn instead that our "dissatisfaction with life is innate and often accurate," and what interests Betts is watching how people and charac-ters act once this realization is made plain. "Nobody," Betts often says, promises "us a rose garden. Or Eden, for that matter" (*StoryQuarterly,* 72). Betts admires the ability of ordinary people to cope with over-whelming suffering and to "do so with real grace. To write about that and not to sentimentalize, to tell the truth as well as the tragic truths, is what I would like to do as a mature writer."[28]

Within the lives of her characters, love is so often the longed-for expectation. And as Anne Tyler remarked in her review of *Beasts of the Southern Wild,* Betts writes superbly about love, not so much about "falling in love" as about the staying power of love. In her first novel, *Tall Houses in Winter,* Betts relates the love affair between the protago-nist, Ryan Godwin, and Jessica, his brother's wife. As the scene unfolded on her work pages, Betts commented in a letter that "while I was not able to capture any of love's real tenderness (ALWAYS THE UNATTAINABLE: WRITE IT ON YOUR DOORPOSTS), it was a good experience to try and to *know* that there was more beauty here than one was able to express. Some people never *know*."[29] Love moves throughout Betts's fiction, and some people fall in love with each other all over again.

Throughout her fiction mortality hovers. Some characters die violently (car wrecks, drownings, gunfire, a backward step into the abyss of the Grand Canyon); some die young from illness, others worn out from age. Mortality, Betts has come to see, is not itself the thing to dread, but instead *waste*. And so her novels and short stories bear out. Lives may end too soon in death—the mother in "The Mother-in-Law," Mary Grace in *Souls Raised from the Dead*—but the lives have experienced little waste.

In "Doris Betts at Mid-Career: Her Voice and Her Art," Dorothy Scura suggests that these major themes have remained central to Betts's fiction "from the earliest published work to the most recent" as she explores their presence in the lives of children and old people, in the dynamics of family relationships and the difficulties of race relations, in the experiences of her characters as they face loneliness, death, and sometimes love.[30] Even though some critics find the allusions at times excessive, most praise Betts's spoken language, which is like overhearing her characters on the bus or in the neighborhood supermarket. Scura finds Betts's prose style "rich, allusive, metaphorical, suggestive, economical, and flexible" (Scura 1990, 163). Furthermore, it is enriched with humor, often pithy retorts. When a local news reporter heard Betts say that the Arabian horses on the farm were substitutes for her children after they left home, he foolishly asked why she didn't simply have some more children. Betts replied, "My memory's not that short." Such humor and determination show up time and again in Betts's conversation and speeches, as well as in the lives of the characters who appear in her novels and short stories.

The Gentle Insurrection and Other Stories

In 1953 Doris Betts won the *Mademoiselle* College Fiction Contest, a prize of $500, and saw her story "Mr. Shawn and Father Scott" in the pages of the August issue. At the same time, Betts was gathering a collection (including the *Mademoiselle* story) for the UNC-Putnam prize, a contest open to graduates and undergraduates from Woman's College in

Greensboro, State College in Raleigh, and the University of North Carolina in Chapel Hill. The judges were Pearl Buck, Marjorie Kinnan Rawlings, and James Street; the prize was $2,000.

With the *Mademoiselle* award in hand, Betts did not want to get her hopes high for a second prize so quickly; she knew that a novel was a more likely candidate than a short-story collection, and she was prepared to forgo disappointment. The worry was unnecessary. Theodore M. Purdy wrote to Rehder in October that there was "no doubt at all" that the Putnam prize went to Doris Betts's short-story collection *The Gentle Insurrection and Other Stories,* as it was the best of the manuscripts submitted. Purdy added that "in spite of the usual taboo about short stories, I wouldn't be surprised if we would sell more by giving the first award to these stories than if we gave it to a mediocre novel."[31]

All three judges were quoted in paragraph-long blurbs on the dust jacket, each ending with a resounding announcement: "I predict an important future for her" (Street); "I feel these stories will receive a splendid critical reception" (Rawlings); "Mrs. Betts is already a first-rate, professional writer" (Buck). In the euphoria of the publication, Betts happily went to Efrid's Department Store in Durham, where an autographing session had been arranged. Flanked by copies of *The Gentle Insurrection and Other Stories* (it sold for $3.50), Betts settled down to greet her public. "And not a soul came all day long. I could have died."[32] Years later a Chapel Hill colleague sent Betts the February 1991 catalog from Andrew Cahan, Bookseller, which listed *"The Gentle Insurrection and Other Stories:* NY: G. P. Putnam's Sons, 1954. First ed. A Fine and bright copy in a striking pictorial dw." The price—$125.

Betts wrote the 12 stories in this collection during her freshman and sophomore years of college. In preparation for publication, four stories were dropped: "The First and Second Walls" (the longest story at 18,000 words), "The Long, Long Day," "My Name is Jacob," and "Our Feathered Friends." In addition, a story published earlier in the Woman's College literary journal *Coraddi* as "Yesterday Was the Last Time"[33] was renamed "The Gentle Insurrection" and became the title story of the collection. Although Betts dismisses them now as worse than the writing her students do, the stories in *The Gentle Insurrection* impressed judges and reviewers. Moreover, they reward rereading.

The two most impressive reviews of Betts's first book praised it highly. Robert Tallant, writing in the *New York Times Book Review,* said that Betts was "already a sturdy professional writer," "a master of the short story form," and "a candidate for an important position among

those concerned with serious and perceptive reporting in literary form of
the Southern small town and Southern people."[34] In the *Saturday Review,*
Evelyn Eaton declared that Betts should be described by the French
word *sérieux,* a word that "does not preclude comedy, but is simply the
word of tribute that nation of individual critics and craftsmen chooses to
give to the man or woman presenting a well-finished, properly polished
piece of work to an equally 'serious' public."[35] Both Tallant and Eaton
saw the heart of the collection as communication: "the difficulty of
achieving real understanding between people" (Tallant); "[the] charged
atmosphere, subtle tensions, and unexpressed anxieties between well-
meaning people who would like to understand one another, but are
hopelessly divided by our human isolation" (Eaton). More recently,
Dorothy Scura described *The Gentle Insurrection* as "a phenomenal work
for a young writer's apprentice effort" (Scura 1990, 169).

The major issues that Betts explores in these stories present vivid pictures of death (7of the 12 have pivotal death scenes in them), illness,
race relations in a small southern town, mothers deserting children, and
children undergoing initiation experience. There are no plots involving
romance or unrealistic happiness, no exotic places, no glamorous characters. Instead people face the burdens of ordinary life as they struggle
against serious odds to survive. In the mill town story "A Mark of Distinction," a man defies the company rules and builds a fence around his
house, which sits in the row of look-alikes, and through this gesture tries
to claim distinction. Some stories do rely on stereotyped situations—the
vise a landowner holds his sharecropper in ("The Gentle Insurrection"),
black-white mores of a small southern town ("The Sympathetic Visitor"), and the "southern mansion" myth ("Family Album")—but Betts
achieves the action the oxymoronic title promises. Characters who
would cause an insurrection by breaking out of their situations or characteristic lifestyle—Lettie in "The Gentle Insurrection," Miss Parker in
"Miss Parker Possessed," for example—only make plans or contemplate
changes. In the end, they resume their everyday responsibility and routine; their insurrections not only are gentle but sometimes are stopped
cold.

Betts's moving insight into old age seems unusual for a writer so
young at the time. In "The Very Old Are Beautiful," Mama Bower has
none of the "insipid beauty which the very young like to envision in
their grandmothers . . . and she wore no fluff of lace at the throat. Lace,
Mama Bower maintained, tickled the nostrils."[36] Betts also succeeds in
writing several stories from a male point of view. In "Serpents and

Doves," Jonathan Sykes (the Old Man), old and sick, lives on the third
floor of the Turner Rooming House because "arthritis had caught him
firmly by the limbs and wrenched them all angrily from place" (*TGI*,
131). As he grows weaker, the Old Man becomes dependent on his hall
neighbor, a tyrannical woman named Miss Paula, and at times is
tempted, like Coleridge's ancient mariner, to tell Miss Paula the awful
story in his life. A prison guard, the Old Man met his nemesis in a man
named Little Nigger, who was on the chain gang because he had murdered his termagant wife with an ax. Pleasant, gentle, joking, he was
almost like a friend to the Old Man until one day Little Nigger "stepped
out without calling, moved over, walked toward the underbrush" and
did not stop when the Old Man called "halt a time or two, and then the
gun went off" (*TGI*, 152). Little Nigger fell dead. Burdened with regret
and now in old age with his unbearable arthritis, the Old Man keeps his
integrity by denying Miss Paula his inmost thoughts. The story ends
with a risky device as the Old Man confronts the Devil. As the debate
ends, the Devil sneers that "there isn't anything else for you, Old Man"
and receives the quick retort, "So what?" (*TGI*, 165). As death comes,
the Old Man imagines himself young and walking upright on depend-
able legs, and his face in death looks as if he were "having a not unpleasant dream," a sight that frightens and silences the dreadful Miss Paula
(*TGI*, 166).

Betts tells other stories from the point of view of children, an adult
going back to moments in his youth, and an omniscient narrator. Frequently the images are most effective. After a sharecropper has just
walked off, his deserted wife sits shelling beans that "made noises
against the pan like rain in the middle of the night when you come
awake to hear bits of it hitting the roof and wonder if the field will be
muddy tomorrow" (*TGI*, 168). This lonely, routine domestic task suddenly links life with nature itself and its consequences.

In "Miss Parker Possessed," Betts portrays a fortyish librarian who
momentarily sheds her public persona—the old maid who attends to
her library duties with perfect efficiency—and reveals an inner self that
longs to declare her love for Mr. Harvey, a bank teller. A glimpse of Miss
Parker's unseemly behavior at the library board meeting—she mur-
mured the word "sex"—presses the members to consider retiring her.
Overhearing their remarks, Miss Parker resumes the demeanor expected
of her. Ironically, in abandoning her "other" self, she sees Mr. Harvey,
not as her longed-for lover, but for what he is—"a balding bank teller
with protruding teeth and a somewhat unpleasant scar along one fin-

ger" (*TGI*, 222–23). Their eyes meet and nothing happens as Agnes Parker, limp with relief, relaxes again into her safe life.

Some 25 years later, Betts creates another librarian, Nancy Finch in *Heading West*, who moves far beyond Miss Parker's timid desires. Nancy changes radically to claim the inner life and sexuality Miss Parker missed. David Holman called Miss Parker's experience "a small tragedy," as indeed it is, and throughout *The Gentle Insurrection*, Betts writes movingly of the sorrows of lost opportunities to love, sometimes even to communicate.[37]

Many characters in these stories lead sad lives because they fail to find love. Fathers die before sons can say the right word, mothers leave their small children without a backward glance, a husband tyrannizes his wife over trivial household matters, and a father bullies his three children. Only in "Mr. Shawn and Father Scott" does Betts introduce a serious religious theme. Mr. Shawn, a vagrant who carries his money in a mayonnaise jar, persistently questions Father Scott's every action. Mr. Shawn finds that the priest gets "so close," but not quite to the heart of things. In the end, when Mr. Shawn disappears, removing at last his harassing presence, Father Scott ironically assumes this questioning role himself and finds the fire of his youthful days as a priest returning. Feeling a moment of ecstasy, he surprises the town's staid ministers by declaring they must "Work, for the night is coming!" (*TGI*, 78). Betts's later fiction will echo this message in resounding ways.

The publication of *The Gentle Insurrection* prompted some interesting events. Victor Gollancz brought out an edition in Britain, an occasion Betts described as "kind of exciting."[38] In "The Sympathetic Visitor" (originally entitled "A Crepe for Her Brother"), Betts told a true murder story and nearly caused a lawsuit.[39] "The Sword," was chosen by Robert Penn Warren and Albert Erskine for their anthology *A New Southern Harvest*, a volume including titles by Ralph Ellison, Peter Taylor, Flannery O'Connor, Truman Capote, and Shirley Ann Grau.[40] In their introduction, Warren and Erskine noted that they had thought "the two major wars in which this country was involved during the period covered by our collection would have had a stronger impact on Southern writing. The wars have, of course, appeared in the work of some of the writers represented, but they do not provide a characteristic subject or background of what, in most instances, we would consider the best performance. So we have here only two stories which involve war, 'The Sword,' by Doris Betts, and 'A Problem in Logistics,' by Harriette Arnow" (*Harvest*, viii–ix).

The Astronomer and Other Stories

All in all, Betts's first book was a remarkable debut. Her next collection, *The Astronomer and Other Stories* (1966), showed her a more mature writer in these seven stories and one novella. Dorothy Scura praised the title selection, "The Astronomer," as the "finest piece Betts had published up to that time" and a piece that "remains a small masterpiece" (Scura 1990, 170). Awarded a Guggenheim grant in creative writing for 1958 to 1959, Betts completed the research and several chapters for *The Scarlet Thread*, as well as a version of "what was then called 'The Learned Astronomer' . . . with the original opening: 'He said to himself on that day. It is all done and they are dead; no one will care.' "[41] Harper and Row bought the novel and the short story collection that included "The Astronomer." Later the collection was "revamped . . . and I did a rewrite on Astronomer, putting it in the version in which it was published" ("Astronomer" Notes). The collection explores a central theme that John Lang, in discussing "The Astronomer," describes as a character discovering his "complicity in evil."[42] That discovery, Betts suggests, may come in experiencing the loss of childhood innocence or in recognizing that some deeds demand recompense.

Point of view in this collection ranges from an adult recollecting a pivotal experience in childhood ("Spies in the Herb House" and "All That Glisters Isn't Gold") to a very old woman ("The Mandarin") to a young black girl joyously engaging in her first sexual encounter ("Clarissa and the Depths"). Betts again relates stories from a man's point of view—Wink Thomas, a small-town lawyer who has all but forgotten his ambitious dreams ("Careful, Sharp Eggs Underfoot"), and Horton Beam, the retired mill worker who is drawn to astronomy and finds instead that he is called to love the unlovely ("The Astronomer"). Not one of these stories ends happily, but some characters do confront the consequences of their actions and acknowledge that actions incur responsibility. Betts is dismayed by people who glibly recount their indiscretions on television talk shows whose audiences respond: "Oh well, everybody makes mistakes." Transgressions are not easy to dismiss. Betts recently said to an interviewer, "This notion that you may not only have to ask forgiveness, but you may have to do some recompense— that you may *do something* to atone for what you have done—does not seem peculiar to me" (Harmon, 58). In Anne Tyler's *St. Maybe*, Betts cites a case in point when the character Ian Bedloe accepts that he "has done something wrong and actually changes his entire life and tries to atone for it" (Harmon, 58). A wink of absolution, a moment of "cheap grace," an explanation drawn from psychological or social conditions or economic deprivation won't do. Recompense, Betts argues, "is an underlying principle of the universe. . . . Something has to be done. People have to act out their repentance in some way" (Harmon, 58).

Betts's most dramatic fictional example of this principle comes in "The Astronomer" when Eva Leeds finds her abortion a deed that defies forgiveness; her recompense is to return to her husband and two children. Ironically, her husband's name is Sion, a variant spelling of Zion. Eva does not make a joyful return "to the city of God" but will, Betts implies, find her homecoming awkward and the years ahead rough going. In this collection, as in all of her fiction, Betts knows that neither people nor fictional characters are authentic until they see the sin in themselves, until they see the beam in their own eyes, until they accept their complicity in evil.

Many characters in these stories lead a bleak existence because they suffer loss, or because they fail to seize the opportunity to live. A brief moment in the "The Mandarin," for example, looks back at the childless marriage of Clarence Applewhite, now long dead and forgotten, and his wife. Their static life together is clearly revealed when Mrs. Applewhite recollects their trip to Europe. There was no whirlwind of dances and no invitation to dine at the captain's table. Instead, they waited "all the way over and back for seasickness which never came. She could hardly remember the crossing. I stood at the medicine cabinet most of the way, making certain we had brought everything we'd need."[43] A similar missing out on life marks Mildred Stuart ("The Proud and the Virtuous"), who invites the guard of a chain gang to bring his men up to her back porch for ice water. What she considers an act of compassion is nothing more than a foolish, and possibly dangerous, gesture. However, the beer-smelling guard does not drive the prison truck up her country driveway but drives down the highway and out of sight. Mildred's magnanimous moment is lost, and her disappointment is acute: "She thought for one wild moment she might burst into outraged tears, like a teen-ager cheated out of a party" (*Astronomer*, 94). She functions as wife and mother, but her real self remains hidden. Her farmer husband notices the curves of his hogs more than those of his wife, and when the children burst in from the school bus that day, they do not notice the pile of melting ice cubes in the sink, want only an afternoon snack, and miss their mother's humiliation.[44] The small-town lawyer Wink Thomas in "Careful, Sharp Eggs Underfoot," after a ridiculous flurry of action, assumes a fetal position at the end of the story while his senile old father calls him Orlando, the name of the promising son long dead, and begs Wink not to cry. Such lives seem little more than the "butt-ends of my days and ways," and the characters, like T. S. Eliot's Prufrock, find that no mermaids will sing to them.

In this collection Betts writes two autobiographical stories, "Spies in the Herb House" and "All That Glisters Isn't Gold," setting both in her hometown of Statesville, North Carolina, amid literal scenes from her childhood. "Spies" also functions as a "regional study of mill town life where bored children resort to the exotic in imagination" as two young girls, on the verge of adolescence, are sure they have found German spies in the abandoned herb house.[45] Their discovery, the girls are convinced, will bring reprisal, and as they separate for their respective homes, they are sure the foreign enemy lies in wait. Betts tells "the oldest, most profound story there is: the story of a fall from innocence to experience, of a passage from a small safe world into a large dangerous one" (McFee, 60). The narration is not from the child's point of view but from that of the adult Doris as she looks back to the days of World War II, when "there was so much I understood . . . valor and patriotism, and the nature of the enemy. . . . The German High Command across the sea had taken an interest in my life and in its termination." The narrative voice ends the story with a lyric glance at the lost past: "Oh, do you see that in the days when the spies were in the Herb House the world was still comprehensible to Betty Sue and me?" (*Astronomer,* 17).

One of the strengths of this collection is the variety of subject matter, such as the backwoods humor in "Mule in the Yard," when an ingenious hiding place for moonshine (inside the emptied carcass of a dead mule) is unearthed by the sheriff. Far more interesting are the serious racial conflicts in "Clarissa and the Depths," where the dynamics of whites and blacks are played out. Clarissa lives in as a hired maid and baby-sitter, renamed "Clarie" because Mrs. Sullivan finds Clarissa "too long a name for the children" (*Astronomer,* 53). Warned by her male kin against all men—black and white—Clarissa finds herself relentlessly pursued. Her desire for love prevails, and she drops the knife she had in readiness for the grocery store delivery boy. Instead, as he slips into her room, she puts her hand "flat where the blade should have been" (*Astronomer,* 66).[46] By far the most impressive of these selections is "The Astronomer," where Betts tells the story of a retired mill worker named Horton Beam who has, like Job, suffered significant loss.

In the summer of 1958, Betts remarked to Louise Hardeman Abbot that she had "turned 'The Astronomer' into a religious book—the point of realization that human relationships are doomed to imperfection."[47] "The Astronomer" finds its source in a series of sermons the Reverend H. Louis Patrick delivered in Betts's hometown church. The sermons were based on the Old Testament prophet Hosea, "who was asked to love an unlovely woman and thereby learned a great deal about himself and the possible love of God" (Ross, 54).

Horton Beam, the protagonist of "The Astronomer," accepts his retirement watch with the inscription "Well Done," returns to his empty house, and, having by chance come upon Whitman's poem "When I Heard the Learn'd Astronomer," decides to study the stars. Horton Beam chooses the stars because they are remote and isolated, but his library excursions introduce him to the myths associated with the stars—stories of King Cepheus and Queen Cassiopeia, of Cetus and the doomed Andromeda, of Perseus and the winged horse Pegasus. These stories complicate his detached stargazing: now he must consider that "Diana's seven nymphs and the women who had nursed Bacchus marched in a sky the Astronomer had meant to keep austere" (*Astronomer,* 166).

His lonely life (he has buried his wife and both his sons and "outlived his grief for all of them," [*Astronomer,* 150]) is interrupted when two people seek to rent one of his empty rooms. After Fred Ridge and Eva Leeds move in, the Astronomer is drawn into their lives. Eva/Eve has deserted her husband and children, is pregnant with Fred's child, and soon disappears at late hours to take up her life as a prostitute in the red-light district. Like Gomer in Hosea, Eva seems to be a harlot to exploit, not a woman to love. Ironically, it is she who urges Horton Beam to study what is close at hand, "draws him out of his isolation," and eventually forces him "to confront the complexities and mysteries of love and sin and forgiveness" (Lang, n.p.). When Eva nearly dies from an abortion, Horton Beam nurses her back to health, finding meaning and love in these acts. Although Fred and Horton themselves are quick to "forgive" Eva for what she has done, she sees the abortion as a deed beyond forgiveness, a deed that requires atonement. So the novella ends with Eva returning home to her husband, Fred wandering off to nameless adventure, and the Astronomer turning back to an empty house where he "and his telescope remain, one to gather dust, one to become dust."[48]

"The Astronomer" did indeed turn into "a religious book." Guilt requires atonement and cries out for divine forgiveness. Betts suggests this pattern through the watch that Corey Knitting Mills presents to Horton Beam. The watch is inscribed with only two words, WELL

DONE!, although the mill used to include "thou good and faithful servant." Now they have omitted those words lest a janitor call the NAACP if, by chance, he got a retirement watch instead of the usual fruit basket. The watch depresses Horton because it forces him, minute by minute, to watch his life ebb. At the end of the novella, Horton insists that Eva keep his watch and tell Sion that an old man gave it to her. The watch inscription, of course, comes from the familiar parable of the talents told in Matthew 25, where the "good and faithful servant" is rewarded because he has been "faithful over a few things." As a result, he will now be made "ruler over many things" and is invited to "enter . . . into the joy of the Lord." By refusing to wear the watch, Horton Beam has, on one level, acknowledged his own "fallen" state. Beam's gesture in giving the watch to a woman who is literally "fallen," hints that her return home to responsibilities may indeed make her "faithful over a few things."

In this collection, Betts explores her primary themes. In "The Mandarin," Mrs. Applewhite, very old and very rich, leads an isolated existence, dependent on hired help, who irritate her. Suddenly, she sees herself as another version of the Chinese Mandarin. Incredibly old and rich, he lives half a world away, the story goes, and you, living half a world away, could by pushing a button kill the Mandarin. His death "would make you rich beyond your wildest dreams; and [if] no one—including the Mandarin himself—would ever know you did it, would you push the button?" (*Astronomer*, 26). Betts finds this moment of human temptation fascinating; indeed, facing such a dilemma, Betts says, "is a good measure of man."[49] It *is* what a person knows about his or her own actions that counts.

In "The Astronomer" Betts explores characters' choices through the image of maps and labyrinths, an image central in *Heading West* and *The Sharp Teeth of Love* because Nancy Finch and Luna Stone clearly change their lives by ceasing to follow a map and enter a labyrinth instead. Reading about Theseus and the labyrinth, Horton Beam ponders "whether life is really a map, where you follow the trails marked out for you, or whether it's a labyrinth" (*Astronomer*, 200). If things are set up by religion or by parental example and rule, Betts suggests, life is preset like a map. Betts's preference is the labyrinth: "Everyone is in here all by himself for the first time and the only time, and he has to make it up as he goes along . . . there is no certainty—ever, as to how he will come out, and he can only learn so much from the map makers" (Wolfe, 168). Those characters who strike out on their own undergo change, and if they do not find uncompromised happiness, the lucky ones find what Betts calls a far more adult condition—cheerfulness.

Beasts of the Southern Wild and Other Stories

When Betts's third collection, *Beasts of the Southern Wild and Other Stories,* was published in the fall of 1973, Jonathan Yardley's reviews in the *Greensboro Daily News* and the *Washington Post Book World* appeared on the same day, Sunday, 7 October 1973. Although the reviews are substantially the same, Yardley addressed different audiences. He concludes the "local" Greensboro review by commenting on Betts's long-standing reputation among North Carolina readers and regretting that "her reputation has not spread far beyond the state line." *Beasts of the Southern Wild,* Yardley declared, is "a splendid book," and should bring its author a wider reception.[50] As if he assumed that wider readership was now a fact, Yardley opened his *Washington Post* review by declaring: "Here, indisputably, is fiction of the first order" (Yardley 1973, 4).[51] Other reviewers agreed. Michael Mewshaw wrote in the *New York Times* that Betts "bears close reading—and rereading—and her collection deserves the attention and admiration one feels sure it will get."[52] In the *National Observer,* Anne Tyler commented in detail on the technical strength in "The Spider Gardens of Madagascar" and praised especially "The Mother-in-Law," where, she wrote, "a household comes beautifully to life—effortlessly, you might say, but that is only proof of how well Miss Betts can write."[53] And Doris Grumbach, writing in the *New Republic,* bore out Yardley's assessment of Betts's reputation and echoed his praise. Grumbach began by saying she much prefers to read novels, and "so when I discover a short story writer who allows me the comfort and amplitude of a novelist, I rejoice. Such a one is Doris Betts, whose name I have never heard before this volume called *Beasts of the Southern Wild*. . . . Her tone is what we have come to think of as 'Southern,' . . . but her style is her own. There are living, suffering persons caught in sometimes ordinary situations . . . which her subtle, rapid prose renders distinctive and memorable."[54]

Betts herself feels that these nine stories "turn a corner. They've bent time a little more; they've bent, or questioned, reality a little more."[55] The range and diversity within these stories represent change and growth, and that, Betts adds, is "the only thing that keeps writers going" (Brookhouse, D3). Mewshaw finds that even though Betts's stories employ "gothic" details, they elude easy categorization. Indeed, Betts's stories "resist interpretation the way Wallace Stevens said a poem should—almost completely," and the collection reflects "very much an index of one woman's intriguing mind" (Mewshaw, 40). Although some reviews criticized the book, saying it used the worst stereotypes of southern gothic, in the main, both local and national responses were positive, quite enough to increase Betts's reputation beyond North Carolina.

Beasts of the Southern Wild was the first of Betts's books to go into a second printing (her modest advance for the manuscript was "about $3,000").[56] Publisher and author were both surprised when *Beasts of the Southern Wild*—along with Cheever's *The World of Apples,* Pynchon's *Gravity's Rainbow,* and Vidal's *Burr, A Novel*—was nominated for the 1974 National Book Award. The judges were Donald Barthelme, James Boatwright, Truman Capote, and Timothy G. Foote. Betts matter-of-factly says that her book would not have been nominated had Boatwright not been one of the four judges. In a newspaper article, Boatwright mentioned that until he introduced the names of Doris Betts and Ellen Douglas,[57] none of the other judges had heard of them. Characteristically, Betts finds such neglect "consistent with what Presbyterianism led me to expect of the world! Recognition is accidental. The achievement of excellence is, I fear, both more important and more difficult" (*StoryQuarterly,* 68).

Written over a period of three years, these stories center primarily on women characters who are unhappy with their lives, and if, unlike Nancy Finch and Luna Stone, these women do not acquire "cheerfulness," they cope nevertheless.[58] Most of these women start out in realistic situations but then float "off into dreams and nightmares and fantasies and myths" (Tyler, 15). The title story, for example, explores Carol Walsh's marriage to a man who sneers at her college education, her love of poetry, and her teaching. To escape her real life, Carol moves in fantasy to become the slave and then the willing lover of a wealthy black man named Sam Porter. When Carol reports her husband's 1:00 A.M. lovemaking as rape, the blacks' "revolution" explodes as Sam and his cohorts (dressed in reverse Ku Klux Klan attire—black suits and masks and cloaks) hunt down and murder Rob Walsh. Although avenged by Sam, Carol Walsh still is his slave and concubine before willingly becoming his mistress. Both men—Rob Walsh, white, redneck, and alive, and Sam Porter, black, cultivated, and imaginary—use women as objects.

Few issues in the South have strained social acceptance more than miscegenation, and in the five fantasy sections, Betts boldly records the stages of white Carol Walsh's falling in love with black Sam Porter.

(Rumor about this part of the plot brought Betts advice to publish *Beasts of the Southern Wild* "under a pseudonym.")[59] Betts's technical skill makes the story shocking "because of the matter-of-factness with which the central consciousness accepts both her real and her imagined worlds and the impingement of each upon the other."[60] The successful creation of the two worlds was certainly confirmed when Betts asked her husband to read "Beasts of the Southern Wild." When he finished, he looked up and asked, "Listen, are you not happy?"[61]

The most ambitious story in the collection (and Betts's own favorite),[62] "Benson Watts Is Dead and in Virginia," explores the use of the numinous as Betts brings together three "dead" people—Benson Watts, the pregnant hairdresser Olena, and a black homosexual named Drum. All three relate how they died, and all wear identical bracelets bearing three admonitions: "To AVOID G.B. [going back], 1. Dwell, then travel 2. Join forces 3. Disremember."[63] These "spirits" carry on the activities of the living—they talk and eat, quarrel and sleep, describe their surroundings, and prepare for the required journey. Initially Benson, a history teacher who died of cancer, is alone in a Thoreau-like cabin in Virginia, far from his native Texas. Here he moves in a virgin wilderness as had the Indians and "creates a surreal world which is at once haunting and convincing."[64] As archetypal beasts (the deer and the wolf) hover, Olena and then Drum join Benson, play out their strange roles, and tell their stories. In a rare moment of humor, Olena longs for her old life in Florida, where by now, she wails, "I could have been married . . . and had regular customers on my sun porch and bought myself a dishwashing machine. . . . I could have joined the Eastern Star" (*Beasts,* 179). Still, their afterlife experience has compensations. The landscape is unpolluted—"no boats or motors, no fishermen, dogs, garbage, foam, signs, fences. No plastic bottles drifting near the shore"—and even Olena, inching closer to Benson, asks him in the dark if it isn't good "not to be planning ahead? Saving money? Paying insurance?" (*Beasts,* 156, 186).

The eight-part story ends not with Olena birthing a baby as she was convinced she would but with her "death." Drum simply disappears. Then Benson closes his ledger book, places it under Olena's arm, and pushes the raft-bier out into the sea. The last sentence is Benson's—and the reader's—rumination on these strange adventures: "Maybe somewhere there'll be someone to read the words, or someone who dreams he has read them" (*Beasts,* 192). Betts says that in this story she tried "to capture that feeling you get in William Blake's poetry that natural objects are almost translucent with eternity on the other side. Here Benson Watts, an agnostic, died, but he actually wakes up to find himself neither in the void of non-existence nor across Jordan on heaven's golden streets. Instead he is surrounded by ordinary trees, briars, and rivers."[65] The story explores an after-death experience where Benson, free of pain and bandages, hospitals and suffering, attempts to discover the nature of this new existence. Warren Leamon suggests that Benson's "life after death becomes a metaphor for the vicious circle of philosophy, the circle in which illusion and reality, mind and matter chase each other endlessly" (Leamon, 67). Neither Benson nor the reader can "explain" what happens in the story, but perhaps Benson's happy sensation of arriving at Thoreau's cabin suggests the possibility "that each of us died away into our personal image of serenity and would be tucked there forever like something in a pocket" (*Beasts,* 156).

Twenty years later, in *Souls Raised from the Dead,* Betts writes another moving after-death experience as Mary Grace Thompson happily follows the spirit of Miss Lila Torrido down the hospital corridor. And in *The Sharp Teeth of Love* (1997), the ghost of Tamsen Donner materializes—some 150 years after her death—to demand answers about the man who caused the disaster of the Donner party. This stepping over into the next life fascinates Betts, and "Benson Watts Is Dead and in Virginia" is by far the most involved and intriguing attempt to render an otherworldly experience, one that can be neither proved nor contradicted.

Betts wrote "The Ugliest Pilgrim" in a 39¢ red stenographer's notebook, making revisions and additions in red or sometimes black ink. When Betts sent this notebook along with other materials to the Mugar Memorial Library, she included a long typed letter that recounts the genesis and development of "The Ugliest Pilgrim."[66] One of her students had planned to write a story about the "ugliest man in the world," and although the story never materialized, the student's idea stuck with Betts. She was intrigued, too, that when even her best students turned their hand to writing a love story, clichés and sentimentality ruined their attempts. In early January 1969, the idea for "The Ugliest Pilgrim" emerged, and Betts soon envisioned the story ending "as Joan Baez ends a song, on a note of piercing sweetness. So it would have to be a love story, probably" (Betts 1969).

The *literal* start of the story was a candy bar. Betts found herself methodically peeling off the outside chocolate of a candy bar and eating the covering first. This mundane action made her think how some people pause before acting, while others do not. Thus the story begins with a girl, Violet Karl, sitting in a bus station eating a candy bar as she ponders a trip. With only two manuscript pages, Betts had "no idea what the story would be . . . but had the vague notion [the girl] was terribly ugly and wanted it changed" (Betts 1969). The name "Violet" may suggest "some sense of 'blushing unseen' or may have come, Betts said, because violets "were blooming in my own yard" during the writing (Betts 1969). Betts kept these early details, and the story of Violet Karl, a deep scar cascading down one side of her face, resulted. She journeys to Tulsa to claim the healing power the TV preacher proclaims. Once in the Hope of Glory building, Violet sees only an assistant who unctuously advises her to seek "inner beauty." What Violet finds instead of physical beauty is love—a paratrooper named Monty. What the glib assistant advised simply to get rid of Violet ironically is the point: she finds inner beauty.

On her journey, Violet fills notebook pages with lists of people and places to praise, intermingling them with scriptural references she copied to prove her need to the preacher in Tulsa. Betts added bits to the story during the rest of April and then set it aside to deal with exams, student papers, and a "flurry of family activity." When she returned to the red notebook, the idea of the story as a folk ballad story was still strong, and the writing "flowed on from that, rather quickly, inside a week" (Betts 1969).

"The Ugliest Pilgrim" appeared first in the winter 1969 issue of the *Red Clay Reader*[67] and then as part of *Beasts of the Southern Wild*. "The Ugliest Pilgrim" has been dramatized several times,[68] and in 1981 Shelley Levinson adapted "The Ugliest Pilgrim" for her Conservatory film at the American Film Institute in Los Angeles. (Didi Conn played the lead role of Violet Karl.) Levinson, on leave from her high school teaching post, directed the 30-minute film, *Violet,* which was produced by the American Film Institute and won an Academy Award as the 1981 best short feature. In accepting the Oscar, the producers acknowledged their debt to Doris Betts.[69] In March 1990 Dorothy Rompalske extended her option for the motion picture rights to "The Ugliest Pilgrim."

In the September 1996, *Violet,* a musical based on "The Ugliest Pilgrim," was given a full workshop version performance at the Lincoln Center Theater. Joe Regal of Russell and Volkening attended and reported to Betts that the performance was moving and the music impressive.[70] Hopes are high that *Violet,* with book and lyrics by Brian Crawley and music by Jeanine Tesori, will make it to Broadway. "The folks making the musical from U[gliest] P[ilgrim]," Betts reported, "just won [a] $25,000 prize for same, so maybe the project will fly."[71] And fly it did. *Violet,* starring Lauren Ward, opened 14 February 1997 at Playwrights Horizons in New York. The ad in the *New York Times* declared the musical "A Blooming Success!" and a blurb from Clive Barnes read: "A truly charming and meaningful new American musical. See it!" Initial enthusiasm has been complemented by awards. The New York Drama Critics' Circle named *Violet* the best musical of 1997. *Violet* is also the winner of the 1997 Richard Rogers Award. Although the musical takes considerable liberty with Betts's text, much of the story's strength remains. Enthusiastic audience response extended the original run through 6 April. Writing "The Ugliest Pilgrim," Betts has said, gave her pleasure; as story and in its varied adaptations, it has given pleasure to readers and to theater audiences.

Other stories in *Beasts of the Southern Wild* invite attention, particularly "The Mother-in-Law," where the wife-narrator's uncanny ties with the dead mother-in-law she never knew intersect the worlds of the living and the dead. Effortlessly Betts shifts into flashbacks to tell the story of the dead woman—her family of three sons, her death from cancer at age 40, her fear that Ross (the afflicted son) will be neglected. These past events merge into the narrator's conscious present life. Married to the son Philip, the narrator faithfully cares for Ross, and assures the ghost of her mother-in-law that Ross is "just fine. . . . He will live a long life" (*Beasts,* 46). The story is a moving "meditation on family love and its responsibilities and failures" and by far "the most moving story in the book" (Tyler, 15).

Beasts of the Southern Wild is Betts's most impressive short-story collection, evidence of her skill and maturity as a writer. The later work has continued to deepen as Betts has entered late middle age. Like the late Walker Percy whom she so admired, Betts continues to be on to something.

Chapter Three

Better Failures:
The First Three Novels

Like Eudora Welty before her, Betts managed to publish a collection of stories *before* a novel, reversing the notion that publishers will take short stories only after a successful novel. At first, Betts was far more comfortable as a short-story writer and looked at novel writing as "a forced action"[1] short-story writers seem quick and even impulsive, novelists slow and more deliberate. This change in rhythm encourages an interest in the changeless, she adds, and in her case has drawn her more and more to the novel form. Although she resisted writing novels, Betts persevered. To critics and reviewers, the later novels far surpass her early efforts, and while Betts acknowledges the improvement, she is inclined to describe even her most recent novels not as unqualified successes but as better failures.

Betts's publishing debut with *The Gentle Insurrection* coincided with her quickly assuming other new roles—wife, mother, then working mother-wife. Until her husband finished law school and entered practice, Betts was, if not burdened, at least dominated by these roles. Then in 1957 she entered a new phase and clearly recognized a true sense of herself and of her reputation. In that year, the young family moved from Chapel Hill to Sanford, North Carolina, where Lowry Betts joined the law firm of Pittman and Staton. Doris Betts began working on the *Sanford Daily Herald,* finished a novel, published it, and, perhaps equally important, claimed her identity.

Not long after the move to Sanford, Betts had an unusual experience, a "double exposure," she called it. Betts was 24 years old, and one day downtown as she walked past the Hotel Wilrik, she had "a strange feeling I have had before and been unable to identify."[2] In the same moment she stood still before the Hotel Wilrik, she also felt she had stepped seven years into the past, was 17 years old, and had paused in front of the Vance Hotel in her hometown of Statesville. "There I walked," Betts explained, "24 $^1/_2$ and 17, all at the same time. And what returned to me was that same sense of I-KNOW-I-will-make-my-way-in-the-world" (Abbot, letter, March 1957). As she continued down the Sanford street, she passed various townspeople, nodding a greeting to them as she went and was acknowledged in return. That afternoon, she was "not merely 24 $1/2$ and a mother and somewhat disillusioned, but . . . also 17 and cocky!" (Abbot, letter, March 1957).

The feeling of "double exposure" came with a rush, bringing a decided sense of well-being Betts described as the "absolute rush of feeling you get in adolescence" when people do seem good. In Sanford, people had been "*wonderful* to me and my gratitude is out-of-proportion, teen-age. It is strange" (Abbot, letter, March 1957). This experience in many ways let Betts leave the past behind. Growing up in Statesville had brought its pleasure and success, but Betts also felt obliged to prove herself to the town. At 17 she felt driven to show the town that "you could come from the wrong side of the tracks and still achieve" (Abbot, letter, March 1957). Now at 24 she was herself, a public figure who spoke at the Rotary Club the week she moved to Sanford (87 members were in the audience). In Sanford, Betts writes in an important letter, "for the first time in my life I am Doris Betts," someone who, Sanford townspeople say, "writes," and "it no longer matters that by 'writes' they mean something different from me, that they are a little suspicious of it. It means that I am here on my own terms, And fine it is, good" (Abbot, letter, March 1957).

Tall Houses in Winter

In this important year for Betts—a coming of age in a way—her first novel, *Tall Houses in Winter,* was published. The *Sanford Daily Herald* ran an article about the occasion with a photograph of Betts signing copies. The novel was long—383 pages—and set in the Piedmont North Carolina town Betts named Stoneville in Stone County;[3] the nearby town is named Greenway, a larger place where the trains came. (Greenway lingers in Betts's fiction as the central geographic place in *The Scarlet Thread,* as the town where Bebe and Jack Sellers were raised in *The River to Pickle Beach,* and as the town Nancy Finch in *Heading West* returns to after her harrowing experience in the Grand Canyon.)

Betts organizes *Tall Houses in Winter* into three parts taking their titles from Anthony Cronin's poem "Apology," which Betts includes as a frontispiece. For those living safe lives in "ordered houses," Cronin begins his poem, it is easy to praise the "dwelling virtues" in the midst of "gentle days"; even the "desert-maddened preacher" has a captive audience he can readily call "to shrive and to shrivel for God." But as the poem makes its turn, it focuses on those whose lives are less than perfect, those who can hardly advocate truth, having never "been true to ourselves." These people fail to achieve great deeds and in the end plead to be judged "by our own compassion." These are ordinary people, Cronin says, who "dunned by our need through the days are unfailingly traitors / in *Sad and Undignified Ways* to each circle of friends." These are the people who "have climbed to the top of TALL HOUSES IN WINTER."

Dorothy Scura calls *Tall Houses in Winter* apprentice work for Betts and notes that "it has a strangely dark tone for a young writer" (Scura 1990, 173). Certainly the poem sets a somber tone for the novel, which opens in the last days of August 1954 when Ryan Godwin comes home to Stoneville after an absence of 10 years. Suffering from cancer, he returns to the place he had left for good, discovers a person to love in his nephew Fen (who probably is his son), and, at the end of the novel, returns to Massachusetts for an operation that may arrest the cancer or, then again, may not. Most of the characters in the novel are, like those in the heart of Cronin's poem, ordinary, "unfailingly traitors" to life's daily demands. Ryan's only brother, Avery, for instance, grows increasingly dull with age. His spinster sister Asa loses the natural charm of her childhood and becomes a pretentious southern lady when she could have been an excellent businesswoman.

Betts recounts the lives of the three siblings, the marriage of Avery to Jessica Maple, the love affair between Ryan and Jessica, and the world of 12-year-old Fenwick, Jessica's son, whose father could be either brother. The "tall house" where the Godwins live harbors southern stereotypes as well as an undercurrent of rebellion that surfaces too faintly to disrupt proper behavior. On a work sheet, Betts constructed a simple three-generation genealogy of the Godwins along with a list of nine minor characters, each identified by role or profession: Miss Cornelia Satterfield, librarian; Miss Clare, distant cousin; The Little Jew Tailor; and Lady Malveena, the black cook. Reviewers generally found these minor characters "carefully eccentric, just enough to make them stick in the reader's mind . . . [the characters] utter too many casually significant remarks."[4] Flashbacks effectively reveal some characters. In one flashback, the tyrannical father, Flambert Godwin (dead long before the action of the novel begins), appears, "oddly disgruntled that she [Asa] might even be brighter than his two sons" and will not let her enter his business as she wanted.[5] "Real estate," he announces, "is a man's job.

There are certainly duties here [in the household] enough to occupy your time" (*Houses*, 91).

In Asa's and Jessica's lives, Betts explores the limited choices south-ern women had in a prefeminist day. After her father died, Asa did enter his real estate business, but she keeps in the background, letting Ian Travis, the nearest thing to an intellectual in Stoneville, carry out most transactions. At home, however, Asa rules. When Ryan comes up the walk, he knows that Asa and Miss Clara are watching through the win-dow curtain as he approaches. The front door is not thrown open in wel-come, and Ryan hears "to his amusement the subdued tones of his sis-ter's voice as she called like a regular gentlewoman bothered on a busy afternoon—'Lady Malveena, will you see who's at the door please?' " (*Houses*, 29). In an emergency, Asa takes charge, making all the funeral arrangements when Avery and Jessica die in an automobile wreck and insisting that "even small Fenwick [not quite two years old] will go" (*Houses*, 345). As Fen grows up in this gloomy house, Asa calls him Fen-wick and spends more time correcting his grammar than loving him.

In Jessica Maple Godwin, Betts creates a minor southern version of Nora Helmer (in Ibsen's *A Doll's House*) and, to an extent, Hedda Gabler. The most moving section by far in *Tall Houses in Winter* is the flashback where Betts narrates the love affair of Jessica and Ryan, assig-nations carried out under the noses of Asa and Avery. Only Lady Malveena sees what is transpiring. Although Jessica seems irresistible to Ryan, she is just a young southern woman of the 1930s who has little education and, worse, little curiosity about the world beyond Stoneville. When Ryan returns to his college teaching post, the affair continues by mail. Jessica writes her letters at a table in the public library, amused at how shocked the straitlaced librarian would be if she only knew of Jes-sica's lover.

But Jessica marries the dull Avery, a marriage that makes her a dou-ble prisoner in the Godwin house, where Asa presides and Lady Malveena manages. Little is left for Jessica to do: "During the day Lady Malveena does most of the work and when I help her I feel like a child being permitted to bake cookies in spite of the fact that flour will soon be all over everything. I belong to a number of young married groups, clubs and things. I go to the library, shop, read. On Saturdays I run the mimeograph machine that puts out our church programs. Sometimes I sew" (*Houses*, 321). She is another doll in a doll's house. The year is 1938, and Jessica's letters reveal an abysmal ignorance of the impending dangers in Europe: "I am afraid I am very unconcerned about the Germans, and whoever it is in Czechoslovakia that Hitler thinks ought to be somewhere else" (*Houses*, 324). Trying to follow Ryan's keen interests, she checks out the library copy of *Mein Kampf* but finds it "such a long book that the prospect of reading it all, from front to back, was too much for me" (*Houses*, 326). Rather than learning about the perils Europe is facing, Jessica indulges in sentimental daydreams: "I keep a Heathcliff fixation, after all these years. I used to write a long story about a little girl who lived on the moor and wanted to learn to play the violin" (*Houses*, 324). And she does not dare to follow her moody lover north and fills her time by reading to shut-ins.

Sick with love, Ryan implores Jessica to leave Avery and Stoneville and come away with him. But Jessica lacks Nora's nerve and does not leave, and she never entertains Hedda's impulse to suicide. She will not risk all for self. Trapped in this small town, Jessica has no mother or any other kin concerned enough to orchestrate her courtship and marriage; furthermore, her choices of husbands are few.[6] When Ryan says that marriage to Avery and life in Asa's house will put Jessica "on stage twenty-four hours a day," Jessica fires back a retort that tells the story of many women's lives. "I've done worse things! . . . How many old women do you think I've lived with? How much of my life do you think I've been nothing but a glorified servant, running up and down stairs for all of them? Do you think I like that?" Jessica knows that in time she "would have been absolutely safe; nothing could have touched me!" (*Houses*, 269). Later, Ryan is amazed that Jessica does not sense intuitively that he, not Avery, fathered the child. But Jessica seals off her life with Ryan and declares in a long letter that the child's "father" will be Avery. "He *is* the father. By my choosing I make him so" (*Houses*, 337). The blazing automobile accident that kills Avery and Jessica saves her perhaps from death by boredom, leaves the little boy for Ryan eventually to love, and leaves unknown Avery's possible suspicions and Jessica's unspoken regret.

The major themes of love, time, change, and mortality dominate the novel, and they continue to absorb Betts. Ryan's illness sharpens his perceptions as he finally discusses death in his long conversations with Ian Travis, and as Ryan experiences deep love for Fen. Betts convincingly creates a middle-aged male protagonist and an equally convincing preadolescent boy, even though female characters were certainly more accessible to a young woman writer. If the minor characters are at times cartoonlike, several nevertheless are memorable. Miss Clara, for example, hears poorly and forever gives a pat answer that fails to fit the question. Her deafness is no tragedy as long as she knows that the next meal will soon be served.

If Ryan Godwin faintly echoes Quentin Compson's complicated view of the South in *The Sound and the Fury,* Lady Malveena is Betts's version of Faulkner's Dilsey. Stereotyped as the faithful and all-knowing servant, Lady Malveena, nevertheless, is the still point in the novel for Ryan and the boy Fen. Although not consciously intended to be stereotypes, Betts says, her black characters were predictable because racial and social conditions in small southern towns were static and she put in her fiction what was at hand. Change lay in the future.

Reviews generally praised Betts's technical skill in her first novel and noted that Betts at times stirs readers to their "own flights of memory,"[7] writes "absorbingly, inventively and all too briefly of a beautiful and doomed love" (Deal, 4). Although the novel was not an unqualified success, Betts had shown that she could produce a readable novel. It was a novel "that promises—and disappoints" (Deal, 4), but Sylvia Stallings declared that Betts "has no need to question a literary instinct as sound as it is gifted."[8]

The Scarlet Thread

Betts's second novel, *The Scarlet Thread* (1964), was first called "Thomas Allen" or sometimes "I, Thomas Allen." Initially the new work centered on pretense, "about man's constant and unending pretending to be things he is not and cannot be until he loses sight of what he is and how—gripe though one may—nothing in our civilization could endure (at least not now) apart from this constant falsity."[9] Betts wrote a prologue in the voice of Thomas Allen (later dropped), a character described in this early phase as "a not wholly admirable man, nothing so good or so likable as Ryan. But, at least attempting to be honest in a stiff-necked way" (Abbot, letter, 1956). The 250-word prologue discusses pretense, which Thomas Allen sees as "the central attribute of complex and intelligent life," something pervasive and inevitable. As the early titles suggest, Betts originally intended to write in the first person, in Thomas's voice, and wanted "to write the book in satire form, but that calls for more maturity than I have. I *do* think tragedy is easier, though I did not once" (Abbot, letter, 1956).

What Betts wrote in the end was *The Scarlet Thread,* a tale of "the material rise and spiritual decline of a family of sharply contrasted individuals," a subject "that has produced some great fiction along with an avalanche of artistically contemptible but commercially successful novels and film scripts."[10] In its three sections, this novel tells the stories of the Allen children, Esther and David, as well as Thomas, for whom pretense is simply *one* flaw. Betts looks back on *The Scarlet Thread* as more a failure than a success, saying the sections of good writing in the novel consti- tuted small short stories embedded in a plot that generally struck review- ers as excessively gothic. Certainly sensational elements abound: the doomed love affair of Esther Allen and Max Carson; a strange sorceress, Miss Bethesda Lee Michael, a little black woman living in a tree house over the Katsewa River;[11] and a midnight ride of the Klan to torture a dignified black man named Big Jube. Silas Bennett (who marries Mil- dred Allen's peculiar sister Rosa) is an alcoholic and lets the gauges in the new cotton mill rise unchecked. An explosion and fire result. In addition, there is a rape, Rosa's imagined pregnancies, a hint of incest, acts of bla- tant cruelty including wife abuse, a severely crippled tombstone cutter named Bungo Mayfield, illegitimate births, and a sudden death that haunts Thomas Allen like a murder. In his review of the novel, William Peden regretted the sensational elements but realized that Betts was still a young writer; "With the gothic excesses of *The Scarlet Thread* behind her," he wrote, "she may yet become a very good one" (Peden, 32).

The Scarlet Thread covers important aspects of North Carolina history. Betts relates the Klan's surge of activity beginning in 1867, farming patterns ("cotton in the ground in March, corn in April. . . . Plow around cotton in May"),[12] the financing and construction of a cotton mill, the early days of the state university at Chapel Hill, and daily life in the rural South as it is mirrored in a small town. In particular Betts traces the evolution of a village farming community into a small town as a cotton mill emerges to change the economic pattern at the turn of the century. The mill came when farmers were poor and unhappy, when both Populists and Republicans had a brief flourish of power in the South, and when racial tension was high because the "Red Shirts revived many of the old Klan methods and there was a race riot in Wilming- ton."[13] Mildred Allen regards the mill village families as subhuman and refuses to let her children associate with them. When the noise of mill construction finally subsides, Mildred shudders to discover that the con- stant noise of the mill machinery in operation enters the very pores of her being. She longs only to escape this environment and years later does so when Sam Allen builds her, at last, a big house in town with money he has accumulated in part through dishonest dealings.

Many sections of the novel are excellent, free of gothic excess. For example, Sam Allen looks down Main Street, and the description of the blighted trees foreshadows the unhappiness that will disappoint the Allen family's expectations for happiness. "Shading his eyes, Sam took a quick east-west look along Main Street. The rutted road was bordered by uneven rows of trees—walnut, wild cherry, mulberry, elm; and two of the tallest ones had some kind of blight, so that even in the green summertime their leaves were halfway dead and the topmost branches scorched and nearly empty" (*Thread*, 22).

Betts creates a memorable character in Mildred Allen's sister. Rosa Bennett is obese, grows larger every year, and constantly imagines she is pregnant. After a family crisis, Mildred leads Rosa into the kitchen, murmuring, "I bet you never stopped to eat." Once in the kitchen, Rosa becomes a skilled and fastidious glutton.

> Rosa's eyes were already darting here and there, to the cabinet where there might be a half lukewarm berry pie or baked sweet potatoes shriveling in their skins.
>
> Mildred set out biscuits, cold bacon, the last of the milk in a jar which still held the coolness of the cellar. She took a tomato off the windowsill and cut it into quarters in a saucer. The molasses and a jar of pickles were still on the table from supper.
>
> Rosa began to eat. She gave no appearance of enjoyment, but cut and spread and chewed with a rhythmic efficiency as if this were a skill she had acquired from years of training. She ate like an eating expert, without interruption or wasted motion, every bite the same size, every morsel chewed the same solemn length of time; until the table was as bare as the fields of Egypt after the locusts passed. (*Thread*, 26)

Another minor character, Cabiliah Henderson, a black deaf-mute, is devoted to Mildred Allen's father, Angus Mackey. Like the old woman in Welty's story "A Worn Path," Cabiliah makes his periodic journey to visit Angus, and the two old men sit, content in each other's presence, finding that silence serves them well. When Cabiliah appears after Angus has died, Mildred finally leads the old man into Angus's room and takes "the tortoise-shell box off the dresser . . . to let Cabiliah see the pocket watch lying there with its hands stopped" (*Thread*, 147). Finally the old man understands and crosses the room to the mirror, where he "cupped both his hands on the cold glass around an image which was not there, and laid one index finger swiftly on the handle of each drawer" before he stumbles out of the house, half-running, letting his sack of precious food slide from his arm to the ground (*Thread*, 147).

This friendship parallels the bond between the youngest Allen child, David, and the crippled tombstone cutter, Bungo Mayfield. Refusing any part of the family's wealth after Sam and Thomas rise to own the mill, David goes as an apprentice to live with the crippled Mayfield, learning by painful blows how to transform marble into shapes and letters and coming to love his crippled and demanding teacher.[14] The enmity between Angus Mackey and his son-in-law Sam Allen counterpoints these two harmonious friendships. Angus takes delight in thinking up schemes to annoy Sam Allen. Like Mr. Fortune in Flannery O'Connor's story "A View of the Woods," Angus attempts to erase his son-in-law's presence, addressing his daughter as if she were a widow—and the better off for being so. At mealtime "Sam Allen had to stop the serving bowls by force or else every vegetable would pass him by" (*Thread*, 13).

Betts individualizes the minor character Big Jube, who demands that his family learn to read. In 1859 Big Jube's father stole a hymnal and taught himself to read, matching the hymns he knew by rote to the strange-looking words. Big Jube copied these hymn words onto slips of paper, repeating "each one over and over until the shape of it was in his mind. . . . When he was sure he had one learned, he filed it with the others in boxes and crocks and jars according to the opening letter. There was no consecutive order, since he had never learned the alphabet" (*Thread*, 185–86). On winter nights Big Jube would draw word slips from jars, spread them on the table, and recite them to his children. When Big Jube read "THE JOO-ELL is in the FOWN-TAN," he shuddered in response, "as if he were having a nervous chill" (*Thread*, 187).

Esther Allen, the strongest and most independent female in the novel, despises housework and bedevils Miss Eliza Tilley, the school-teacher who forces her fondness for maxims upon her students as "exercises in parsing and penmanship and as punishment for the girls" (*Thread*, 48). Esther copies the maxims reluctantly but relishes one, "Circumstances alter cases," so much that Miss Eliza regrets the whole business. When the northerner Max Carson arrives to oversee the mill construction, Esther falls in love with him and sleeps with him. His eventual transfer to Kentucky—a plan that does not include Esther—prompts her to run away in the night. She leaves the scarlet scarf she has laboriously knit for Max trailing from her bedroom window. Mildred Allen associates this act with Rahab's scarlet thread and the spies before the destruction of Jericho (Josh. 2:18). She reads the Scripture countless times but can never clearly understand the connection. Over the years Sam Allen conducts searches for Esther but finds no trace of his daughter. At the end of the novel, Esther (now Mrs. Andrew Warner) returns to Greenway for a day in 1920. Keeping her identity to herself, Esther learns what has become of her family in the long years since her girlhood.

In *The Scarlet Thread*, Betts portrays women who rebel and who suffer. Ernestine Foxx Allen, Sam's first wife, helped raise her brothers and sisters. From the minute Sam married her, she turned "so lazy she never ate an apple that did not drop off the tree into her apron" (*Thread*, 38). Although Ernestine was barely 18 years old, she was worn out from doing for others and now, safely married, planned just "to sit down" (*Thread*, 38). Neither Sam nor the reader can figure out how she got up the energy to comb her hair and run away "with a man from Alabama" who traveled the countryside selling his wares (*Thread*, 39). Ernestine's escape is one of the happier episodes for women in the novel.

Totally different from Ernestine, Mildred Allen silently accepts domestic responsibilities. She cares for her old father at home and at the same time protects her husband's ego. Mildred never questions *her* duty and despairs because Esther refuses to learn the skills all women are supposed to master. Mildred warns Esther that "when you get grown, no man will have you! Can't cook, won't work and never stop talking! When I was your age, I was running a whole house and my mama was under her tombstone!" (*Thread*, 86). Yet on the very day of this lecture, Esther copes all alone when her grandfather dies.

Headstrong, Esther loses interest in school when she hears Charles D. McIver's speech at the Stone County Courthouse. McIver declares: "Educate a woman and you educate a family" (*Thread*, 294). The old-maid teacher, Miss Eliza, finds McIver, "Magnetic, Just Magnetic!" but Esther says that if she gets an education, she wants "it to be for my own sake" (*Thread*, 294). Her independence sets her apart, and later many gossip that Esther ran away from Stone County and her family as a fallen woman.

Many women in the novel are disappointed in their lives, and several suffer at the hands of men. Thomas has his way with the mill girl and then abandons her. Even the likable David Allen gets the Mayberry girl in trouble, and Sam Allen spends a lot of money to move that whole clan to South Carolina. When Thomas Allen marries Nellie Grimes, he claims the Grimes home place as his own, even to the very bees in their hives. When he humiliates Nellie on their wedding night, she learns too late that she married the wrong brother. But just as Jessica marries Avery in *Tall Houses in Winter,* the deed is done, and Nellie is left to bear children—10 of them—and to endure a miserable marriage.

Sam Allen pursues dishonest ways and finds them easy, beginning with the homemade brew, stored in jars and hidden beneath the floorboards, which he sells in Hobbs's Store. Later, it is easy enough for Sam to keep two sets of books, cheating Hobbs and starting Sam's own financial rise until at last he owns the mill. Thomas follows his father's ways, and the thoughtlessness of his youth turns into adult cruelty.

Too many plot lines are put in motion, but *The Scarlet Thread* is ambitious and interesting because it depicts an entire social scene in the midst of rapid economic change and follows its principal characters from adolescence into adulthood. What Betts describes as small short stories embedded within the novel show her narrative skill, even though the whole fails to measure up to the parts.

The River to Pickle Beach

When *The River to Pickle Beach* appeared in 1972, Jonathan Yardley (then book editor of the *Greensboro Daily News*) praised Betts in his *New York Times* review and declared (as he did when *Beasts of the Southern Wild* was published the next year) that the time had come for her audience outside of North Carolina to increase substantially: "Among those Southern women who have contributed so vigorously to postwar American fiction, Doris Betts has never quite got her due."[15] *The River to Pickle Beach* justified Yardley's hope for that wider recognition. Set in the tumultuous summer of 1968, Betts's third novel juxtaposes the assassinations of Robert Kennedy (on 4 April 1968) and Martin Luther King Jr. (on 4 June 1968) with the violence carried out in the lives of ordinary people living in a quite unremarkable place, an off-the-beaten-track beach on the North Carolina coast. Although Yardley finds the local "violence as a microcosm of national violence . . . rather strained" (Yardley 1972, 12), other reviewers thought that Betts successfully conveyed "the violence in the air" that swept the entire nation, a violence that "permeates this tragic tale" from the childhood trauma of Jack Sellers to the brutal murders of a retarded mother and son as the novel ends.[16] *The River to Pickle Beach,* Yardley wrote, has "the ingredients of good popular fiction" but also is "serious and provocative." Yardley thought "the portraits of Bebe and Jack Sellers are first-rate" and found the novel extremely well written (Yardley 1972, 12). In retrospect, if the advertising budget had been greater, the timing perfect, and the booksellers more enthusiastic, it is possible that Betts's third novel might have been a best-seller. But it wasn't. Nevertheless, the *National Observer* did list *The River to Pickle Beach* as one of the 20 best novels of the year.

In the 1970s, Betts called herself "an unaffiliated theist,"[17] and if her religious stance was less secure then than it is now, Betts still sought pattern and meaning. *The River to Pickle Beach* takes place in the summer of 1968, Betts told an interviewer, "because that was a year that shook the country hard, when people searched for the answers to those basic questions. . . . The human mind has trouble going on without any meaning at all. It wants a pattern, shape and some kind of coherence" and *"Pickle Beach* is about what happens when the meaning is taken away" (Plotkin, 2A).

The assassinations of John Fitzgerald Kennedy (on 22 November 1963), Robert Kennedy, and Martin Luther King Jr. shocked the nation, and the American public learned firsthand that terror and violence can happen *here,* not just in foreign places. These murders entered homes because television carried live coverage and countless reruns. In the living rooms of ordinary people, tragedy played across the screen, and the American public watched the horrors of assassinations, just as they watched the nightmares of the Vietnam War during the dinner-hour evening news. The endless details in television reports, both of the murders themselves and of the effects upon family survivors, invited an unjustified familiarity between victim and viewer. Television coverage allowed viewers to consider these national figures as if they were neighbors just around the corner. Betts's character, Bebe Sellers, watches the television screen and calls out: "They shot Bobby Kennedy just like the president." "I wonder where Jackie is?" "And Ethel Kennedy with another baby coming."[18]

Bebe assumes this familiarity; however, the complex web of international politics and terrorist acts eludes her. On the morning of 6 June 1968, the television announced that Robert Kennedy was dead and quoted from Sirhan Sirhan's notes that "Kennedy must die by June 5. Jordan and Israel were the cause of it, whatever that meant" (*Beach,* 83). Bebe, like other viewers, eventually finds the constant television coverage tiring, and finally she "was worn out with it. They could shovel him under any place by now—she'd be relieved. Oswald and Sirhan had begun to look alike" (*Beach,* 92). To break the strain, Bebe drives to her neighbors, only to find their television blaring away. Her neighbor Willis is more interested in the clear picture of his new set than in the tragedy on the screen. Such superficiality is commonplace, but Bebe does see that her response to the fate of the Kennedy family is simple-minded. As Betts shows throughout the novel, Bebe lacks sophistication. She has not been to college, and books do not interest her. Her understanding of the world and her basis for judgment come from the movies she saw growing up, movies of the 1940s and 1950s, which she now watches again on television reruns. Nevertheless, Bebe has common sense, knows injustice and foolishness when she sees it, and seriously tries to adjust to the social climate of a changing South. All in all, Bebe Sellers is one of the most appealing characters Betts has created.

Three epigraphs emphasize underlying themes in the novel. Lines from Robert Louis Stevenson's "The Merry Men" speak of the seeming innocence of the sea, which yet contains magical and dangerous and mysterious wonders, while familiar lines from Eliot's "The Dry Salvages" speak of time as destroyer and preserver. Finally, a line from Ecclesiastes 1:7 depicts the full cycle: "All the rivers run into the sea; yet the sea is not full; unto the place from whence the rivers come, thither they return again." In these early novels, Betts uses the Catawba River, which runs through Iredell County, finally converging with the Enoree River in South Carolina as it joins the sea. Renamed Katsewa in Betts's novels, the river is magical and dangerous and, like time, a destroyer and preserver, linking past and present horror in *The River to Pickle Beach.*

As a boy in Greenway, Jack Sellers lived with his drunkard father, his disturbed mother, and his siblings in a small shack where the river wound just below the sagging back porch. On stormy nights, Jack's mother listened and said to her children, " 'There goes the river,' as if the river were a freight train . . . now coming, now passing, now gone" (*Beach,* 43). And one day when the father, drunk and singing, waded in the river to wash, Jack's mother waded in, too, and axed the abusive man to death as Jack watched from his perch in a tree. Years later, when he and Bebe spend their first night as managers of George Bennett's rental property at Pickle Beach, the sound of the ocean links with the sound of the river in Jack's mind. The title of the novel might more literally have been *The ROAD to Pickle Beach,* but it is the river that winds through familiar towns to the ocean, bringing Bebe and Jack Sellers to a new phase of their existence and linking them with other people and events that alter their lives.

The novel opens on 15 May 1968 when Bebe and Jack Sellers leave their jobs in Durham and move to Pickle Beach; it ends on 25 June 1968 in a manhunt for Mickey McCane, a man Jack knew in the army, whose paranoia makes anybody different from him the enemy. The novel comprises 17 chapters, averaging about 20 pages each. The narrative voice centers on Bebe in 9 chapters, Jack in 6, and Mickey in 2. Mickey also appears in subsections of 4 other chapters, and the beach neighbor, Pauline, in 1.

The longest section of the novel (chapters 7 and 8, which cover 124 pages) relates Bebe's trip alone back to Greenway to see her family. Through this visit and the family picnic–grave-cleaning reunion, Betts portrays the "new South" in a small southern town. Racial tensions emerge with Bebe's two brothers: Troy is a liberal; Earl was George Wallace's campaign manager in Stone County, where the Cotton Club is a euphemism for the KKK. In Greenway, progress is measured by Gold Medallion homes equipped with every new gadget and by old homes that in the 1960s metamorphosed into smart boutiques or antique shops.

The sensational elements in *The River to Pickle Beach* are graphic and more realistic than gothic. Madness drives Jack's mother, Serena Mae, to commit a grisly murder and years later to kill herself. She "screwed out the light bulb and laid it neatly on the shelf where they kept sheets and towels for the insane, so the closet was black-dark at the end; . . . there was plaster under her fingernails where she raked a hand down the wall while she choked . . . and died" (*Beach,* 174).

The psychopath, Mickey McCane, had a wretched childhood. First one and then the other parent disappeared for weeks or even months, coming back at last only to fight again, not to be reconciled. When his mother did bother to put him to bed, Mickey was to hold his breath for the count of five before he let it go. But the count didn't put him to sleep, and he heard the taxi, every time, pull up to the curb to carry his mother off to yet another fling. Sexually frustrated, he convinces himself that Bebe desires him and begins a relentless pursuit to prove the fact. Late in the novel, he puts on his army camouflage suit, takes his high-powered rifle, and shoots George Bennett's in-laws, a retarded woman and her son (the "Pinheads") as they sit happily in literal innocence, tossing a ball between them in the gentle waves of the ocean's shore. To Mickey, the delight and pure love these two find in each other is unnatural and disgusting, a sight that must be removed from his world.[19] Mickey is so maladjusted that he recoils at the sight of goodness in *any* form.

In contrast to Mickey McCane's sexual frustration and soured marriage, Bebe and Jack are happily married. (Some reviewers thought Betts detailed "too many peeps into the bedroom where Bebe and Jack, over and over, demonstrate their compatibility" [Bitker, 4].) Bebe is not common or flighty, and if she is not book smart, she has common sense. Betts creates a moving scene when Bebe realizes that Foley, a college dropout, is teasing her beach neighbor Pauline about religious matters. Indignant, Bebe lights in. "Go on to Chicago, Foley Dickinson! . . . You ride right on and you be sure to play smart aleck everywhere you go, hear? Talk down to everybody. Do it in Latin. Mock people's religion! . . . You know what's wrong with you, little stuck-up boy? You don't think you'll ever do anything dumb or mean or ugly. You don't think you'll fail or be ashamed or have something in your past you can't stand to look at! You think taxes and laws will solve everything. Well let me tell you something!" (*Beach,* 381). Almost in tears, Bebe knows she lacks the words to express how difficult it is to understand other people. The scene ends with Foley's bashful apology and laughter among the three. Often Bebe describes herself as simpleminded, but she knows mockery for what it is, and with Jack has found what many never do—happiness, comfort, and love.

The reunion visit to Greenway furnishes a contrast between Bebe's past and the present life at Pickle Beach. She takes a taxi from the bus station to her mother's house at 217 Connor Street, a street like Newton and Rickert and Armfield, located near the Allen Cotton Mill. Bebe's old neighborhood was on the wrong side of the tracks, the last section to get paved streets, and one that needed ice delivery longer than other neighborhoods. As a young girl, Bebe's dream was to live on the other side of town in one of the big quiet houses whose doors had oval panes and balconies above the porches. But home in Greenway was always in a mill house, and Bebe's father Walt (as had Doris Betts's father Bill) had run a spinning frame in that mill. Now the rich Allens were gone, buried in a gray mausoleum that looked for the world "like a ginger-bread house that had molded in damp weather" but made of Italian marble "so the Allens might wait out eternity in finer quarters than their neighbors" (*Beach,* 191). Years earlier, Bebe had pointed out to Jack the brass plate on the mausoleum door where family members from *The Scarlet Thread* lie buried—"Thomas and Nellie Grimes Allen, Mildred and Sam. 'One daughter ran away and was never heard from again,' she said" (*Beach,* 191–92). And in that instant Bebe knows she too will run away from home, eloping with Jack Sellers.

Even though Bebe and Jack were both raised on the wrong side of the tracks in Greenway, they differ sharply. Jack is hungry for knowledge, especially about plants and trees; he devours books about them and learns their Latin names. Bebe doesn't even look at pictures in the Audubon book. Her entertainment and her models for life are pre-1960s movies. Foreign films, as well as recent American ones, disturb her, and Bebe confines her movie watching to reruns of a safer era. She watches the films of World War II, whose message declared that if people just held on long enough, everything would be all right—Walter Pidgeon would come home to Greer Garson—love stories, and movies where Fred Astaire and Ginger Rogers danced and danced.

Movie plots and actors fill Bebe's daydreams and fantasies. In an imaginary café's back room, Bebe cooks while drunks pass by who may not notice that her legs "are on loan from Betty Grable" (*Beach*, 8–9). She closes her eyes, and there is "Burt Lancaster making love to a woman on a flat beach in the moonlight," or there is Jennifer Jones drowning "in a storm at Land's End, just beyond reach of Joseph Cotten's hand" (*Beach*, 3). During the Durham years, Jack works on the grounds crew at a local college and catches what he can of professors' lectures as he passes open classroom doors or windows. Bebe works her waitress job and every day longs to abandon apron and customers to "eat at the Stork Club, the way Anne Baxter did" (*Beach*, 33). In a recurring daydream, the death of the hero is averted because Bebe comes to the rescue. She plays her favorite fantasy again and again. Bebe, a young guerrilla leader, fights cruel Nazis as she leads her brave comrades over rocky slopes. "Beautiful as Ingrid Bergman and wise as Pilar," Bebe listens as a man shows her how to shoot a rifle and then asks if she could now kill a man. With all the drama that fantasy can muster, Bebe replies, " 'Mechanically, yes, . . . emotionally, I don't know.' Bebe was proud of that dialogue. Once this had been a long dramatic speech; by now she had pruned it until everything was in those six words and the intense way she spoke them" (*Beach*, 319).

Near the end of the novel, before he joins the manhunt for Mickey McCane, Jack tries to put a pistol in Bebe's hands. When she cannot touch it, Jack leaves it on the hearth, yelling back from the yard for her to lock the doors. Bebe is to "stay out of sight and shoot out and shoot through" (*Beach*, 386). As Bebe looked at the gun, she knew Jack had almost asked her if she could kill Mickey McCane if she had to, and she knew she had come very close "to answering like a movie" with her six well-rehearsed words (*Beach*, 386). Mickey eludes the men, and when Bebe sees him approaching, she aims at his middle. Unlike a movie heroine, Bebe does not shoot because, she tells Jack later, "I didn't know how" (*Beach*, 390). Her killing the psychopath would have been too sensational a way to end the novel, and Betts leaves him to be captured by the sheriff and his men offstage. The novel ends as it began—with two ordinary people who, in this new place, unwittingly stumble into a dreadful double murder and survive. When the crisis of the manhunt is over, Jack says simply, "I love you, Bebe." And Bebe responds, "Yes, you do" (*Beach,* 390).

One particular strength of the novel is a host of excellent minor characters. Foley Dickinson, an upper-middle-class college dropout and example of the 1960s youth and rebellion, appears at Pickle Beach. Miss Whitaker, the formidable black nurse in charge of the Pinheads, at first intimidates Bebe and pesters Jack, but with Foley Dickinson, her considerable good spirit emerges. She yells to Foley, "Is black beautiful?" When Foley quickly retorts, "Well, in your case it has to strain some," Miss Whitaker roars with laughter, declaring to Jack that "this boy doesn't have any of our hangups" (*Beach,* 315). And the grief that overwhelms Miss Whitaker when her charges are murdered is moving. Bebe's mother Grace, her brothers, their wives, and the large extended family who appear for the reunion show a small southern town in the late 1960s. Intellectual pursuits are rare; progress is measured by better cars and air-conditioned houses. Social change is slow, and the inner longings and secrets of the heart go unspoken.

Technically *The River to Pickle Beach* is impressive. Readers who found the flashbacks in *Tall Houses in Winter* competently done, but mechanical, must admire the skill with which Betts modulates the plot into the past and back again. With Jack's knowledge of plants and Foley's extensive reading, Betts can indulge herself with allusions to Audubon and pickerelweed (Jack), to ecology and semantics (Foley). While Bebe imitates Alice Faye in "Alexander's Ragtime Band" as they walk along the beach, Jack and Foley outdo each other as they write in the sand: *Mollusca, Arthropoda, Chordata, Amphibia.*

In *The River to Pickle Beach,* Betts probes the notion of evil, a theme central in her fiction. The blatant murder of the Pinheads is the most obvious manifestation of evil at work, but it is insidiously present in the lives of many characters. Jack Sellers has early on suffered its consequences, and the opening lines of chapter 2 begin with a stark meditation on evil: "There may be something evil inside the world, always threatening to break loose, under pressure and searching out weak spots in the crust. Something inimical to human happiness. Jack Sellers had good reason to believe that this was true" (*Beach,* 25). That force breaks through in meanness, madness, and murder in this novel, in the cold cruelty of Thomas Allen and of the KKK in *The Scarlet Thread,* in the calculated moves of the kidnapper Dwight Anderson in *Heading West,* and in the sinister pair who scar the fingers of a young boy and turn him into a prostitute in *The Sharp Teeth of Love.* Betts knows well that the forces of evil are present, waiting to erupt. Flannery O'Connor shared the notion and, anticipating the denial from the secular world, often quoted Baudelaire's familiar line: "The devil's greatest wile is to convince us that he does not exist." In Betts's fiction, evil forces exist and threaten human happiness.

Chapter Four

Heading West and East: The Later Three Novels

Heading West

In July 1971, Doris and Lowry Betts were among 10 passengers who rode the rapids down the Colorado River—225 miles through the Grand Canyon. Guided by professionals, the group entered the river at Lees Ferry and emerged at Diamond Creek. Betts sat in the bow of the raft, a position washed over frequently by waves, often 25 feet high. Although a hat protected her face from the intense sun, Betts suffered severe blisters on her shoulders that became infected. Among the side trips on the river run was the Silver Grotto, and Betts, who does not swim, put on a life jacket and took her turn, pulled by a rope across the deep lake in order to see the interior of the grotto below. Betts did not have a kidnapper for company on this trip, as does her character Nancy Finch in *Heading West,* but like that character, Betts suffered physically from the ordeal of the Grand Canyon experience. More important, like Nancy, Betts saw in the strata of the canyon walls "the history of the earth before [her] eyes."[1] Because the novel is set in the western landscape and because for the first time a "strong single woman is at the center of the action," *Heading West* (1981) marks several major shifts in Betts's novels.[2] The landscape details of the rural and small-town South establish place in Betts's early novels, where male characters—Ryan in *Tall Houses in Winter*, Sam Allen and his two sons in *The Scarlet Thread*—dominate. Although Bebe Sellers is the central character in *The River to Pickle Beach,* she is not the complex, ironic, interesting person Nancy Finch turns out to be.

Heading West was a Book-of-the-Month Club selection, a stroke of good fortune that ensured sales. Writing in the *Book-of-the-Month Club News,* Clifton Fadiman may well have persuaded members to order Betts's novel rather than the alternate title for the February 1982 selection, William F. Buckley Jr.'s *Marco Polo, If You Can.* Fadiman zeros in on the theme of evil in *Heading West,* seeing the novel as a "study in what

Coleridge, describing Iago, called 'motiveless malignity.' "[3] Betts's novel, Fadiman argues, escapes the banal characteristics of the "psychological thriller" and instead is a novel "truly psychological in its moral insights, truly thrilling in its interlace of suspense and surprise" (Fadiman, n.p.).

The novel does have the elements of a cliff-hanger or a romance. On vacation with her sister and brother-in-law, Nancy Finch falls victim to a random kidnapper in the Blue Ridge Mountains near Linville Falls. Armed with a loaded gun, Dwight Anderson takes Nancy first toward Florida and then, for no reason, heads west. Various adventures ensue, and the climax occurs against the spectacular walls of the Grand Canyon when Nancy, having escaped, begins her descent only to be followed and then found by Dwight. Inexperienced as a hiker and weakened by the heat, Nancy sees Dwight approach. When she lifts a rock to throw at him, he takes a reflexive step back and, crying out a single "No," falls into the abyss. Nancy nearly succumbs from heat and exhaustion but is rescued from the canyon and then rescued again by Chan Thatcher, a chance acquaintance and a resourceful woman, who nurses Nancy back to health. Hunt Thatcher, thinking at first that she is exploiting his mother's habit of taking in the needy, in the end falls in love with Nancy. As the novel comes to its close, Nancy has returned home to Greenway, faces the past and her own flawed self, is ready to marry Hunt Thatcher and, once again, to head west.

Heading West enjoyed good sales, a movie option followed, and the novel received far more critical attention than had Betts's previous titles. However, in August 1983, sales had come to a virtual standstill. Mary Maguire, an assistant to Robert Gottlieb, wrote Betts that Knopf would soon partially remainder *Heading West,* retaining 234 copies in warehouse storage and offering 7,000 for sale at a 75 percent discount ($3.25 a copy).[4] By 1986 the only title by Betts in print was her third collection of short stories, *Beasts of the Southern Wild,* and that only in an anthology, *3 by 3: Masterpieces of the Southern Gothic,* sharing billing with collections of short stories by Shirley Ann Grau and Mark Steadman.[5]

In contrast to this discouraging impasse, by the 1990s, the status of Betts's books had changed radically. *Heading West* came out as a handsome Scribner paperback (with a cover that Betts says brings *Thelma and Louise* to mind), and Louisiana State University Press reissued *The Astronomer and Other Stories* in 1995. Betts's novel *Souls Raised from the Dead* (1994) went to a third printing in hardcover and then came out in a paperback edition. In November 1996, Scribner Paperback reissued her third novel, *The River to Pickle Beach*. With its reissue in paperback, *Heading West* gained a new audience.

The reviewers of *Heading West* found the characters strong and the writing skillful, especially the buildup of suspense. Gary Davenport praised the use of landscape as Betts pushes her characters out of the South and into the West, where the land's vast openness "parallels the growth of Nancy's independence," and where the "interlaced bushes and thick trees" of the southern landscape symbolize the restricted and stifling life Nancy led with her family in Greenway.[6] Edmund Fuller commented that beneath "its dramatic suspense," *Heading West* presented "a web of characters rich in subtle moral and psychological ramifications."[7] *Publishers Weekly* called it "a fierce novel," one that dealt subtly "with relationships, with love, with America and its values."[8] Reviewers were impressed with the depth and range of allusions that Betts introduced in the text through her well-read librarian character, Nancy Finch. Literary allusions come from childhood reading (*Hansel and Gretel, Little Women,* Nancy Drew mysteries), from British writers (Shelley, Blake, Wordsworth, Chesterton, Auden, Lewis, Green) and American writers (Whitman, Melville, Twain, Faulkner, Warren, O'Connor, Updike). Paul Tillich, Reinhold Niebuhr, Karl Barth, and Thomas Mann are alluded to, as are classical figures (Sisyphus, Persephone, Niobe) and biblical characters and events. Beth Gutcheon wrote in her *New York Times* review that Betts "may or may not be familiar with Blondie, but without doubt she is deeply familiar with the Bible, Flannery O'Connor and William Faulkner, Freud, Darwin, Konrad Lorenz, Navajo mythology, and the doctrine of Manifest Destiny."[9] As one reviewer quipped, Betts does seem to know *everything*.

If some readers find the plethora of allusion too heavy, others are intrigued by the sheer amount of information Betts conveys in these pages. Readers learn about raising wolves, flying helicopters, reading tarot cards, gathering supplies for a hike into Grand Canyon, hauling house trailers, riding horses, tending the sick and dying, searching for missing persons, raising a child with California-style indulgence, conducting auctions, developing farmland into commercial property, lying, and finding one's true self. After Harvey T. Jolley, a disgraced Tennessee judge, links up with Nancy and Dwight as yet another hostage, the trio's adventures allow Betts to bring to life many details of middle America. As the three travel, they stop at various trailer parks alive with bingo games as well as at roadside restaurants and motels where waitresses and desk clerks can't tell kidnap victims from quarreling couples.

Reviewers generally found the first part of *Heading West* well done. Indeed, Jonathan Yardley described this part—which he sees ending on page 215—as "brilliant" in depicting Nancy Finch's journey into her dark night of the soul, a process of real self-discovery.[10] Betts, however, should have ended the novel at this point, Yardley argues, and because she does not, she "reveals herself to be a short-story writer who is uncomfortable going long distance" (Yardley 1981, 3). Of all reviewers, Yardley was the most critical of the remaining 144 pages, which he sees as a second novel "in which the same woman is nursed back to health, falls in love, and returns home to accomplish her final liberations" (3). Yardley calls the latter part of the novel "superior women's-magazine fiction" (3). In a review of *Heading West* for the *Southern Quarterly,* Mary Anne Ferguson echoed Yardley's position in slightly less damning language: "In marrying her [Nancy] off to the son of the female rescuer who is a role model for Nancy, Betts has ended on a weak note."[11] Love and marriage are simply not an acceptable conclusion, these reviewers suggest, for a novel in which the main character has "headed west," has "lit out for the territory," has broken her life pattern. Choosing a traditional social role won't do.

Betts anticipated this criticism. In an interview, she conjectured that "there's probably going to be a lot said in *Ms.* magazine because Nancy . . . is able to find happiness with a man. It's a love story in a way, and it's kind of hoaky, but it's not hoaky to me. The book does deal with themes of liberation because, at the end, Nancy makes some fundamental decisions *for herself,* based on *her* experience. She has learned about herself, and not through any political or organized means."[12] In Betts's judgment, Nancy set out as a Pharisee; by the end of the novel, she is a Publican.[13]

Nearly 15 years later, the Yardley review came up in an interview, and Betts elaborated on her thesis that women often are changed by seeing *themselves:*

> Yardley really would have preferred . . . that Nancy went down in the canyon where she had an experience of existentialist despair, and the novel left her there. He felt that to bring her out, certainly to have her get married, which seems neither feminist nor liberated, and then to come back home and deal with her awful family turned a literary novel into what he called "women's fiction." I do know what he means. I wrote him and just said, "I haven't learned how to do that well enough yet." . . . If it feels like *Cosmo[politan]* or *Redbook,* then I haven't done it yet; I've copped out.[14]

Although Betts contends that she respects Yardley's review, it still troubles her. The experience Nancy Finch undergoes in the Grand Canyon, Betts says, attempts "to say something about suffering and compassion—Nancy . . . did learn something. The canyon made her able to be generous. And if that's just 'women's fiction,' God, I'm going to have a hard twenty years ahead!" (Ketchin, 257).

Betts, and doubtless many readers, do not think that love and marriage completely stop a woman's freedom, no matter how many reviewers say they do. In her essay, "Doris Betts's Pilgrims," Peggy W. Prenshaw quotes Rachel Brownstein on the goal of the heroine: "What the female protagonist of a traditional novel seeks—what the plot moves her toward—is an achieved, finished identity, realized in conclusive union with herself-as-heroine. Her marriage or death at the end of the narrative signifies this union. . . . The aim of the female protagonist of a novel *is not a husband but a realized identity*" (emphasis added).[15] And Prenshaw applies Brownstein's argument to *Heading West*: "Nancy Finch's western pilgrimage may have led her to an old-fashioned wedding, but she made her way with the courage to mark her own trail . . . and she did so with eyesight sharp enough to see the bogs and sloughs all along the way" (Prenshaw, 83). Because Nancy Finch and Hunt Thatcher know they are far from the ideal partner each has dreamed of, they will marry as much for a safeguard against loneliness as anything. Trapped in her life in Greenway, Nancy had longed for romance and exotic cruises, but dreams rarely come true.

In his review "The Fugitive Hero in New Southern Fiction," Gary Davenport called *Heading West* a "fine novel" and further saw Nancy Finch as a classic example of that "paradoxical fate," being a southerner. Southerners, he suggests, exist "at the intersection of two deeply rooted conflicting traditions: on the one hand stand family piety, southern Protestantism, regional loyalty, and attachment to the land; and on the other stands ornery rebelliousness" (Davenport, 440). During the flight halfway across the country in the kidnapper's company, Nancy manages to make several telephone calls, yet none are quick and direct calls to summon help. Instead, she calls former lovers, a strange artist who works in the Greenway library, and family members. Obviously Nancy is not "really interested in being rescued," and Davenport sees her telephone calls as a chance "to explore her relationships . . . rather than to summon help" (Davenport, 440).

Set a southerner down in New York, and he or she may feel like "a paroled convict" or "a deposed monarch"; set him or her down to a family Sunday dinner in Birmingham or Raleigh, and he or she "may well experience acute feelings of suffocation and entanglement" (Davenport, 440). On one level, Nancy Finch comes to terms with her suffocating life when she discovers that her quasi-invalid mother and her brother, Beckham, (a bit slow and living with more-or-less controlled epilepsy) have, like the family of Gregor Samsa in Kafka's "The Metamorphosis," "thrived rather than languished in her absence" (Davenport, 441). Unlike Kafka's traveling salesman, Nancy does not cling to a sentimental photograph, and she does not scuttle away to die while the family bustles about with life. She dies neither in the Grand Canyon nor at home. Instead, she discovers that she is not indispensable. If she has been a bird in a gilded cage, part of the entrapment was of her own doing. As the spinster daughter, Nancy lived at home, looked after her mother's and brother's needs, and, in the process, let them grow increasingly demanding and dependent.

For all her feelings of being the martyr, what Nancy Finch finally sees, Betts has said, is her true self: "she's no more righteous than her irritating kinfolk." Like Ruby Turpin in Flannery O'Connor's story "Revelation," Nancy "dimly realized she might *be* a wart hog from hell."[16] As the novel progresses, Nancy Finch comes to know clearly where she has been and then begins to discover where she is and what she can do.

Many reviewers made a connection between *Heading West* and Flannery O'Connor's story "A Good Man Is Hard to Find." O'Connor's family of six, like Nancy, have their vacation plans interrupted by a villain, one of those mysterious criminals of our age who emerge, as Dorothy Scura notes, "from nowhere to wreak seemingly unmotivated violence" (Scura 1983, 7). But Scura and others should not equate Dwight Anderson with O'Connor's Misfit. Anderson (alias Melrose Lee Shelton, whose real name is Ervin Childers) is, as Fadiman described him, an example of "motiveless malignity." It is true that O'Connor's Misfit directs the murders of Bailey and his wife, the children June Star and John Wesley, and the unnamed infant and then shoots the grandmother three times in the chest. But far from being the mysterious criminal Scura describes as "colorless and inarticulate" who shows up on television as a strange kidnapper or Tylenol poisoner, O'Connor's Misfit talks passionately (Scura 1983, 7). Obsessed with spiritual longing, the Misfit, O'Connor says, may someday become the prophet he was meant to be.[17] Dwight Anderson shows no trace of spiritual distress and is instead an enigmatic force of evil loose in the world. He does not wage the interior battle of the Misfit, who longs to know the truth of the Resurrection, verification that to him would make all the difference.[18]

As she does in *Souls Raised from the Dead,* Betts balances the danger and terror in *Heading West* with humor. Once, when Nancy manages a call home to Greenway, a strange voice answers the telephone. When Nancy asks, "Who is this?" the jewel of a maid—never had they employed one while Nancy was at home—responds, "Whom are you calling?" I've been replaced, Nancy says to herself, "with a grammarian!"[19] As Nancy suffers and survives, she sheds her old identity and her habit of always being sensible. "Every dress I own," she says, "is in a color that won't show dirt!" (*West,* 188). Late in the novel, Judge Jolley, back home in Sommerville, Tennessee, gets the notion that he is a mulatto. Irritated with his groundless suspicion, Nancy says, "You're a boring Anglo-Saxon like the rest of us. . . . I know black is beautiful nowadays but there can't be many rewards in Tennessee for changing color" (*West,* 305, 307). In this novel, Betts is at her comic best.

In part 4 of the novel, Nancy comes back home to Greenway after side excursions to hear Judge Jolley's version of his release and to discover Edwin Childers, the twin brother of Ervin. Nancy finds her family ready to use her as they have in the past, even though the household routine has changed. There is the new maid they could never afford, money (Nancy never knew about her father's life insurance), a new Buick (her mother could drive after all if the car has automatic steering), and Beckham's job at the auction house. Then the family forms the Blue Bird Corporation to develop and subdivide the grandfather's farm. On the surface, loose ends are neatly tied up to make satisfactory solutions for the Finch family, but a closer look suggests that the changes were *always* possible. When Nancy's kidnapping altered their routine, the Finches were quite able to change and even to see after their own welfare. As Esther Allen learned in Miss Eliza Tilley's country schoolroom, "Circumstances alter cases."

For all the strength in the comedy, in the host of characters (major and minor),[20] and in the lyric descriptions of landscape, the notion of evil is at the heart of *Heading West.* It's easy enough to see evil in Dwight Anderson, who, early in the novel, jumps his car onto the sidewalk and nearly crushes a boy against a building because he ran a nail down the side of Dwight's car. Dwight's flat "huh-huh" laugh does not suggest amusement, and when either Nancy or Judge Jolley asks why he commits violent deeds, he retorts, "Why not?" The absence of a motive makes his personality baffling, his evil deed inexplicable.

The heart of the novel, however, lies in exploring the evil not of Dwight Anderson, but—as Betts has frequently commented—in Nancy Finch herself. Freed from her whining and exploiting family, Nancy becomes a willing partner in the kidnapping. She recalls the thousands of meals she has cooked for her mother and brother Beckham and thinks about her sister Faye, who, their mother always says, was the pretty one. Even the men in Nancy's past have been disappointing—weak or boring or married. She is a spinster librarian, a small-town southern martyr whose life dwindles under the family's needs.

In the Grand Canyon, her dramatic moment of existential despair is prompted not by the fear that she may die but rather by the realization that she has the capacity to commit evil. In Dwight Anderson she recognizes her own dark self. Recovered from the canyon ordeal, Nancy cannot tell even Hunt how, as Dwight moved toward her, "nothing but luck sent him over the edge in advance of her pushing hand." Even now "she could not separate laughter from roaring, as if the cries of lion and hyena had been electronically mixed and repeated and played on her vocal cords loud enough to start the rock avalanche under which he eventually lay" (*West,* 296). And if Nancy ever does tell this part of her adventure, the recital must include not only the death fall of Dwight Anderson but also "the barbaric pleasure with which she had watched him fall" (*West,* 259). Nancy Finch begins her journey as a kidnap *victim,* simply a more dangerous stage of her lifelong pattern. Nancy starts out with "that pious self-pity that giving women get, when they are victims . . . [and] collaborate with the victimizing," Betts told an interviewer; what Nancy Finch learns in the heat and indifference of the Grand Canyon is that she is "no saintly martyr and she *could* kill any sonofabitch who drove her crazy" (emphasis added).[21]

When Betts signs copies of *Heading West,* she claims kin with Nancy Finch and often writes: "To one Pharisee learning to be a Publican." It's not an inscription for "women's-magazine fiction."

Souls Raised from the Dead

Thirteen years after the publication of *Heading West, Souls Raised from the Dead* appeared in the spring of 1994; with few exceptions, the book enjoyed praise from reviewers and quickly went to a third printing. By December, Simon and Schuster was promoting the paperback edition, placing *Souls* in "the great Southern literary tradition of writers like Faulkner, Flannery O'Connor, and Eudora Welty" and calling *Souls* a "contemporary classic."[22] Reviews in major newspapers[23] did not go quite that far, but they found much to praise, especially Betts's writing about the death of a child without producing "Little Nell Lives (Only to Die Again)" (R. Brown, 7). Without a trace of false sentiment, Betts has 13-year-old Mary Grace Thompson die, an event that is "neither a made-for-TV movie nor a manipulative tear-jerker" (Ascher, 5); it is an event that "could have descended to the realm of maudlin melodrama" but "never does" (Warren, 5C).

In the *Christian Century,* Jill Pelaez Baumgaertner reviewed *Souls Raised from the Dead,* along with *Millroy the Magician* by Paul Theroux and *Knowledge of Angels* by Jill Paton Walsh. These novels focus "on formative events in the lives of three girls on the brink of adolescence," and all "explore spiritual themes."[24] However, Baumgaertner found that only Betts's novel was convincing as it explored "the arguments for and against the presence of a god concerned about and connected with human triumph and failure" (927). Theroux and Walsh focus on a culture of disbelief searching for something to hold, but Betts presents "a convincing picture of a modern family dealing and not dealing with the death of its youngest member" (Baumgaertner, 927). "Mary Grace Is Going to Die" is the title of Rosellen Brown's review of *Souls Raised from the Dead* in the *New York Times,* but when Betts came to the point of the writing the child's death, she had great difficulty doing so. "I thought maybe I could find a miraculous cure or something," Betts said in a telephone interview, because "I was very fond of her. What happens is you write a lot of dreadful descriptions of sky, you change the subject, you bring minor characters into the foreground. Finally, I thought, 'This is ludicrous,' and it didn't take two pages to write the scene. After that, the book went very smoothly."[25]

The origin of *Souls Raised from the Dead* may be found in many places, but certainly the address Betts delivered during the 1982 lecture visit of Billy Graham to the University of North Carolina campus is of primary importance. In her "Faith and Intellect" speech,[26] Betts alludes to Madeleine L'Engle's essay "The Day Is at Hand," where periods of spiritual doubt are described as "an attack of atheism . . . just as if it were the flu." This same "spiritual flu" comes to Tacey Thompson in *Souls Raised from the Dead,* and her Damascus Baptist Church faith is sorely tested when her young granddaughter dies. Often asked if she based Tacey on herself, Betts says that she and Tacey are "the same age, and we've experienced a lot of the same things, seen the same wars. So, yes. I guess a lot of Tacey is me."[27] The point of Betts's novel is theodicy or, as Rabbi

Harold Kushner expresses the matter, *When Bad Things Happen to Good People*. "God never pretended," Betts says, "that people get what they deserve in life."[28]

Juxtaposed to the theological basis of Betts's novel is a mishap in everyday life that provides the central metaphor. The event literally occurred on Highway 15/501 outside of Pittsboro where Betts lives, a connection rather inelegantly described in a headline of the *Durham Herald Sun:* "Chicken Truck Wreck Spurred Idea for UNC Professor's Latest Novel."[29] Chickens whose feet had never before touched ground and whose wings had never been called upon to function wandered in disarray upon the highway, lighting in bushes and trees and even upon the blue light of the highway patrolman's car as he tried to "bring order out of chaos in a tableau both horrible and funny" ("Whispering Hope," 80). Betts describes the look on the patrolman's face as "existential despair." Frank Thompson's struggle to impose order finally succeeds—the injured driver is taken to the hospital, other officers arrive to redirect traffic, the cleanup goes forward—and the moment of chaos passes. Francis (Frank) Thompson, a highway patrolman for 12 years and single parent of Mary Grace (the mother, Christine, ran off with the Orange County tax collector when the child was barely 10) soon faces chaos that he cannot control. Routine tests following Mary Grace's fall from a horse reveal a life-threatening kidney disease, and Frank, who longs to keep this child from harm, can neither protect her nor save her from death.

The mindless and scattered chickens in the opening scene, as Betts comments when she reads from this novel, ironically introduce the prevailing religious theme—Christ's lament over Jerusalem, whose children he would have gathered "together, even as a hen gathereth her chickens under her wings" (Matt. 23:37). "For me," Betts told one audience, "the story began: Tell chicken truck wreck: End of chapter—can't protect."[30] The novel, Betts says, "is not about how the daughter survives her illness and is raised from the possibility of death, but about how a parent can go on after such a blow, about how the FATHER'S soul can be raised from the depth of despair" (Hubbard lecture, n.p.). Late in the writing of the novel, Betts met and heard the Nobel Prize poet Czeslaw Milosz and found in his moving poem "With Her" the thematic epigraph for *Souls Raised from the Dead*.[31] This poem, Betts has said, was like the chicken wreck—fortuitous, lucky, like Grace ("Whispering Hope," 84).

Other events were influential. In 1981, Leighton Frederick Sandys Ford Jr., son of evangelist Leighton Ford and a nephew of Billy Graham, was a junior at the University of North Carolina. Intelligent and gifted,

Ford was one of Betts's advisees. He was also a promising distance run-
ner, and as he crossed the finish line in a race, he suffered a heart attack
and died following open-heart surgery. When the young die first, that
death "is probably what shakes your faith the most."[32] Even for a deeply
religious family such as the Fords, the son's death was surely difficult to
fit into "the picture of a benevolent God," Betts assumed, "because it
would have been hard for me, as it has been hard for people down
through the centuries" (Bost, B9). For a time, Betts corresponded with
Leighton Ford, and in sharing the grief in Sandys Ford's death, Betts
found connections for the death of her character Mary Grace Thompson.

For assistance with the technical medical information, Betts went to a
friend, Chapel Hill physician Dr. Bill Blythe, who became her consultant. Blythe (son of the North Carolina writer LeGette Blythe) proposed
that Betts use kidney failure as the disease to be dealt with in her novel
because, he said, "we can cure almost everything else" ("Whispering
Hope," 80). Betts does not allow the medical detail to overwhelm the
reader, but she does not flinch from the tiresome and often grim proce-
dures that Mary Grace endures as the disease worsens. In her notes for
the novel, Betts lists the tedious steps involved in the dialysis procedure,
as well as diet restrictions for the patient. Mary Grace knows, for
instance, that ice cream and jello must be figured into her daily allowed
liquid intake.[33] From the first signal that routine tests must be repeated,
to the diagnosis of chronic renal failure, to dialysis (first on a machine
and then with a postdialysis kit at home), to periods of reprieve, to ever
more alarming symptoms, to a successful kidney transplant, to pneumo-
nia, to death, Betts moves with ease and skill through hospital corridors
and operating theaters, and with sensitivity among the members of a
heartbroken family.

Another page of notes includes the origin for the title of the novel,[34] a
summary of the characters, and specific background details about the
Thompsons. "Local genealogists claim the Thompson family has, in its
family tree, (though unproved) the poet who wrote 'The Hound of
Heaven,' and that Frank has unintentionally been named for him"
(Notes, n.p.). In the novel, the Thompson kin send Layla Thompson to
England to trace the family history. Layla's efforts produce a photo-
copied book—$12 per copy—that she sells during the Fourth of July
reunion picnic Mary Grace nudges into being. Some in the family hoped
Layla would find nobility in the early generations, but the most distinguished fact she uncovered shows "a tentative branch toward poet Francis Thompson, who was said, in a footnote, to have written a famous

Christian poem in which Jesus, like a hunting dog, ran eternally after the scent of human souls."[35] Even in Layla Thompson's homely terms, the "hound of heaven" undergirds the novel, pursuing those whom he will, as the faith of Mary Grace's kin is thinned and tested when she falls ill and dies.

Although "The Hound of Heaven" is the most obvious Francis Thompson poem to associate with the plot of *Souls Raised from the Dead,* Betts's notes include a copy of another Thompson poem, one concerned with the death of a child—"To Monica Thought Dying." The poet Francis Thompson found his closest friends in the poet Alice Meynell and her husband, Wilfred. Thompson delighted in the Meynell children—Monica, Everard, and Viola—who, in turn, were particularly close to him. In a letter to Wilfred Meynell written in October 1891, Thompson told of glancing through the newspaper when a notice "gave me a 'turn.' My eye strayed carelessly across the announcements of deaths, and suddenly saw—'Monica Mary.' My heart stood still, I think. Of course the next second I knew it must be some other Monica Mary."[36] The newspaper experience prompted Thompson's poem, which expresses deep grief because he momentarily *thought* Monica Meynell was dead. When Frank Thompson's daughter dies, it is not some *other* Mary Grace, and the grief of father and grandparents lasts.

Betts makes Frank Thompson a believable and sympathetic character, but his relations with women make up a curious aspect of the novel. He marries Christine Broome because she lies about being pregnant. Now divorced, Frank has two women friends—Cindy Scofield, a newspaper reporter, and Jill Peters, a younger woman, Mary Grace's riding instructor. Frank's assumptions about women irritate feminists, who, at the same time, admire his devoted care of his daughter. When, for example, the doctor insists that Frank watch the dialysis procedure in order to help Mary Grace, Frank looks about the clinic and observes that "there were some jobs women were biologically fitted to do while men were not. He didn't see any male nurses putting needles in arms here or unclogging people's tubes!" (*Souls,* 217). Men, Frank argues, are not cut out to be schoolteachers or nurses. He genuinely cares for both Cindy and Jill, sleeping with first one and then the other, but he outrageously describes the arrangement as having a good chiropractor on each side of town. When, on bended knee, he proposes to Jill Peters, he does so because the marriage would give Mary Grace a woman to talk to. Furthermore, he is positive that once Jill marries him, she will abandon all notion of becoming a veterinarian and "find herself pricing sewing machines and carpets. The change would surprise her" (*Souls*, 227). Jill, however, does no such thing and, right or not, is unwilling to give up her own career to assist Frank and Mary Grace. Her relationship with Frank, as Jill puts it, got too heavy, just broke down.

Cindy Scofield, on the other hand, can give practical help. When Mary Grace dies, Cindy steps into Tacey's house and immediately greets callers, makes lists of food and flowers people bring, squeezes Frank's shoulder when she passes his chair. At the end of the novel, Cindy is still sleeping with Frank, and Betts ends the plot without revealing whether Cindy will relinquish *her* aspirations—she intends to move from the Chapel Hill newspaper to bigger publications in Charlotte and then in New York—for Frank's domestic world.

As in her previous novels, Betts populates *Souls Raised from the Dead* with characters who, for the most part, are not university trained, who do not hold prestigious jobs (Dandy retired as manager of the shoe department at Belk's), who are nonintellectuals (the only readers in the novel are Mary Grace, Cindy, and Jillian Peters), and who are ordinary blue-collar folk like Georgia and Virgil Broome. "It's very easy," Betts remarked, "to underestimate such people. I dislike the way they're often portrayed on television, especially in the South, as no-nothing rednecks."[37] What continues to interest Betts is that ordinary people—though lacking the vocabulary to express themselves—struggle with the same profound questions about life and mortality that engage intellectuals. In Frank's success as a single parent, his devotion to Mary Grace, and his patient way with his parents, Betts honors in Frank, she says, "down-the-street courage" ("Reason," 14A).

Betts has created some of her most effective minor characters ever in this novel. There are moving scenes between the two sets of grandparents, who, in spite of their social disparity, share secrets from the past (Dandy and Georgia had a fling years ago), and all four of them despair over Christine's irresponsible behavior. In Christine's absence, Tacey sees about Mary Grace's daily needs, and even Georgia (who has taken to reading palms) acts and judges decisively. When Christine (the logical donor) whines that a kidney transplant is never a guaranteed safe thing for "either, ah, party," Georgia explodes at her daughter—"Shoo, Christine!" (*Souls*, 253).

Betts offsets the tragedy and grief in the novel with humor as she proves to be "essentially a comic writer, no matter how heart-rending her story may be" (Wilson, 5D). She portrays Christine as the "bad mother" who abandons husband and child without a moment's regret to find her calling in cosmetics, which she promotes over her radio pro-gram, "Tina's Arena." Christine's feckless behavior does have its amus-ing side. When she demands to know if a news photographer has gotten her "good side," Christine misses the barbed reply: "I don't know. . . . Which one was it?" (*Souls,* 167). Whenever Christine speaks, she ends with her signature, "OK?"—an ironic choice because the events in the novel move toward grief and lives are far from "OK." Andrew (Dandy) Thompson's tiresome jokes seldom amuse anybody. But his banal efforts are little more than a defense against the fear of his granddaughter's death—and his own.

The centerpiece of the novel, the reunion picnic, has the usual rela-tives gathered amid tables laden with food, but the traditional family ties are compromised because ex-wives and ex-husbands appear with their current partners, causing uncomfortable and amusing confronta-tions. Relatives may not be surprised to find the family history for sale at the reunion, but several purse their lips when Christine hustles sales for her beauty products.

Much of the sardonic humor comes from the limitations or the poor taste of these ordinary middle-class American folk and their world. Farms have given way to tacky strip shopping malls, and the American dream is not a long struggle to earn a better job but arrives in the fourth-class mail announcing sweepstakes that promise instant "good luck and a bright future" (*Souls,* 66). Dandy enters every contest that comes along, and his prizes are the useless clutter of modern-day life: "a kitchen radio shaped like a fat green pepper . . . six tapes for which they owned no tape player" (*Souls,* 70–71). Christine may know appropriate cosmetics, but her inte-rior decorating is tacky—"screaming colonial wallpaper and red draperies . . . hung under the fake walnut arch" (*Souls,* 12). Frank's coworkers Mar-lene and Harold superficially explain that violence in Carrboro and Chapel Hill is caused by "niggers" and suggestions from TV programs. Even the English major, Cindy Scofield, misuses the verbs *lie* and *lay:* should Mary Grace die, she says, Frank would just "lay down and die himself" (*Souls,* 182). These characters do not live in exclusive suburbs, and some even lack ambition. Frank and Mary Grace live in a modest apartment complex called, pretentiously, Ramshead Chateaux; Christine for a time lives in a Florida trailer park with a marine named Nolo; and Virgil Broome will take food stamps in payment for odd jobs and has probably "never paid a dime in income tax" (*Souls,* 236).

At the heart of the novel is Mary Grace, who wistfully imagines her absent mother is the perfect role model, leader of the Brownies, and

proud parent of a marvelous child. But as her illness progresses, Mary
Grace figures out that Christine is *not* going to be the willing donor of a
kidney (an old gun wound keeps Frank from that role) and resigns herself to fate. At times, Mary Grace may seem too well read and too
mature, but in fact she *is* "filled with the odd combination of wisdom
and naïveté, expectation and world-weariness that children of her age
have" (Wilson, 5D). She is fully believable in scenes with her friend Kay
Linda, in episodes with both sets of grandparents, and in scenes with her
horse, Chancy. (Socially and financially, Mary Grace doesn't fit in with
the girls who take riding lessons and own horses, but she does odd jobs
around the stable and briefly enters this world.)

Mary Grace is surrounded by "a conspiracy of good cheer" as her
father and grandparents struggle to maintain an optimistic outlook, but
in spite of their efforts, her symptoms grow more acute and she dies
(*Souls*, 260). The ghost of her neighbor, Miss Lila Torrido, holding aloft a
plate of fudge, appears to Mary Grace and mysteriously and gloriously
leads the dead child down an empty hospital corridor into the light.
"The reader," Baumgaertner argues, "never doubts the reality of Mary's
final vision. . . . This is a profoundly religious novel which turns religios-
ity on its head" (Baumgaertner, 927).

The end of the novel, like the beginning, involves a wreck, not an
unrealistic plot twist in the life of a highway patrolman. In the second
wreck, a car plunges into the Haw River, killing the mother and seriously injuring the 14-year-old daughter. Frank Thompson directs the
rescue, evidence that he has survived in spite of the deepest grief. The
events in Betts's novel confront the question Dostoyevsky asks in *The
Brothers Karamazov:* "How can a person explain theologically the suffering of children? How can we accept the God who refrains from interced-
ing on their behalf?" (Baumgaertner, 929). The answers are not easy,
and all the intercessory prayers in the world did not keep Mary Grace
from dying or her father's heart from breaking. In this family, churchgoing is left exclusively to Tacey, and even her faith is tested. Francis
Thompson's "The Hound of Heaven" hovers in these characters' lives,
a reminder of Christ's pursuing his creatures even in their grief and disbelief.

Tacey, who gives no outward sign of her "spiritual flu," arranges for
the tombstone that will rest on the grave of Mary Grace Thompson.
Tacey selects words from Psalm 30 that speak of suffering and spiritual
hope: "Weeping may endure for a night, but joy cometh in the morning." Frank Thompson's strength and recovery are perhaps best con-

firmed in his ability to receive the hysterical late-night telephone calls from the guilt-ridden Christine as he lets her "talk and cry" (*Souls*, 338). One of the responses to *Souls Raised from the Dead* came from Betts's former University of North Carolina colleague James Devereux, S.J., whose letter ends: "Last night I got a desperate call at 4 A.M., and I thought of Frank and his growing patience with his wretched wife and her telephone calls. I don't mean to say that your novel is a moral tract. Just because it isn't, it touches the heart and makes its way into the reader's life."[38]

"We can all breathe easier," Barbara Ascher declares in her review. "The South has not, as rumored, become homogenized. Doris Betts reports from the front and it is still most particular" (Ascher, 5).

The Sharp Teeth of Love

Betts's sixth novel, *The Sharp Teeth of Love*,[39] impressed her editor Ann Close, who thought that even in the first draft, the novel was well done. Joe Regal at Russell and Volkening found that the revisions Betts completed in the summer of 1995 strengthened the narrative line; the agency was pleased with the novel's prospects and sent a copy to Ron Bernstein of the Gersh Agency in Hollywood to oversee movie rights.[40] The novel emerged from another trip west, this time as Betts accepted an invitation to speak to the Western Literature Association when it met in Reno.[41] Her journey into the Arizona landscape of the Sierra Nevada and the Donner Pass gave Betts ideas for *The Sharp Teeth of Love*. The brief time in Reno, Betts says, was "like a visit to Babylon"[42] with the mirror-lined hotel corridors, one-armed bandits, gaming tables, nightclub entertainers, hotels called Circus Circus, and mom-and-pop grocery fronts transformed into speedy wedding stations called "Silver Bells" and "Love Bells Chapel." The glitter of Reno didn't tempt Betts or Madeline Lunatsky (Luna) Stone, the main character in the novel; instead, it is the dire story of the Donner party that captivates both of them.

Eighty-seven people set out for California. Led by Landford Hastings through a "shortcut" that altered their route, they were trapped by massive snowfall in the Sierra Nevada in the winter of 1846 and forced to eat their own dead to survive. Tourists at Donner Lake State Park can learn the grim details (butchered bodies of women and children, kettles of human blood, etc.) related in various brochures and a film, a dreadful tale that has been the subject of poetry by Ruth Whitman and fiction by Vardis Fisher and others. In her novel, Betts concentrates on Tamsen

Donner, who, before she became George Donner's third wife, had
taught in Elizabeth City, North Carolina, and planned to start a school
once the party reached California. As the journey grew more arduous,
Tamsen's books, journals, poems, wildflowers, and drawings were discarded, left along the trail as if too cumbersome to consider. When she
could have gone out with a rescue party along with her two children,
Tamsen Donner chose to stay with her husband, George. Suffering from
an arm riddled with blood poisoning, he would, as Tamsen knew, die
within hours. Stubbornly abiding by her marriage vows, Tamsen remained by his side, and he did indeed die the next day.

The Donner party wagons had left Springfield, Illinois, on 19 July
1846, finally struggled up to Donner Lake the last week in October, and
on 21 April 1847, the last survivor—the man who cannibalized Tamsen
Donner—was taken out (*Teeth*, 79). By coincidence, Luna Stone and
Steven Grier leave Chapel Hill bound for California and Steven's teaching
position and arrive in Reno on *21 April* 1993. Instead of marrying Steven
as planned, Luna finally sees enough of his outright deception and dishon-
esty and begins her own journey. It is not as dangerous and disastrous as
what Tamsen Donner experienced but changes Luna's life nonetheless. In
the story of Tamsen Donner, Betts saw the metaphor she needed. Tamsen
had experienced a love that required too much sacrifice and submission. In
an absolutely futile gesture, she stayed with the dying George and as a
consequence died herself. She was literally eaten by a remaining member
of the party, devoured, as it were, by love ("Remarks").

In her relationship with Steven Grier, Luna Stone almost succumbs to
what Betts describes as "control-love," but Luna escapes. Steven constantly elevates his academic life and demeans Luna's talent. "You," he
says to Luna, "can do your drawing anywhere. You don't need an insti-
tution, a faculty, a university library. You don't need grants" (*Teeth*, 33).
She finds not only her independent self, but also love for a nearly wild
boy named Sam and for a man named Paul Cowan, who is going deaf.
For Luna, however, love is not pure sacrifice, but something that gives
and requires both gain and loss.

Whereas Betts set *Souls Raised from the Dead* in Carrboro, outside
Chapel Hill and the University of North Carolina, *The Sharp Teeth of Love*
begins in the midst of academe—Steven Grier receives his Ph.D. in
botany, and Luna Stone (having survived anorexia and a mental break-
down) earns a degree in studio art. As Luna and Steven leave for California, they take a nostalgic loop through the campus and the town, look

at familiar landmarks, and then head west. Although Betts uses the dramatic setting of the Sierra Nevada well, the ghostly visits of Tamsen Donner to Luna Stone, rather than the landscape, dominate. At the end of the novel, Steven Grier is left in California, and Luna begins a new journey with Paul Cowan as they head east for life on his family's farm in Wisconsin.

Effective flashbacks tell the story of dysfunctional couples: the Griers (the husband is a heavy drinker) and the Stones (divorced), who have severely harmed their children. In Major Martin Stone (United States Army, retired) Betts creates a monster. He is the "bad father" and altogether as destructive as Christine in *Souls Raised from the Dead* and a good deal more culpable than she. Christine simply never grows out of her childish mentality; her selfish actions are not motivated by cruelty. Martin Stone's are. When he looks at his short, dark daughter, he frequently says to his wife, "Are you sure she's mine?" He warns Madeline (she makes Luna her "call name" when she starts school) that anyone as short as she will probably grow fat and often sends her to bed without supper. When she was 11 years old, he packed her off to "a fat girls' camp in Vermont" because "if I didn't quit eating ice cream . . . I'd soon weigh as much as he did" (*Teeth*, 249–50). Luna's anorexia is hardly surprising. The parents' bitter divorce leaves their daughter withdrawn, and finally she goes where Carolina students go—"to South Wing when their compass breaks. There's always a Bedlam, a Bellevue" (*Teeth*, 89). The theme of abuse comes in a different and dreadful form when the "wild child," Sam, enters Luna's campsite near Donner Lake Park, having escaped from the men who have cut his fingers and forced the wounds to heal in ridges to make Sam a more valuable child prostitute.

Paul Cowan has not suffered child abuse, but a construction blast has permanently damaged his hearing. The experiences of the three characters curiously bind them together; they are all, Luna says, "damaged goods," capable perhaps of honest affection because of their suffering. Their chances of happiness on the Wisconsin farm are enhanced because of Paul's strong mother, Erika. However, Paul and Luna know that rehabilitating Sam will be difficult and risky, just as their own marriage will, in many ways, be a matter of chance. Of the marriages "between the deaf and the hearing," Paul matter-of-factly warns Luna, 90 percent end in divorce (*Teeth*, 331). Love may not be the ever-fixèd mark for Luna Stone and Paul Cowan, but they know at least that love brings losses as well as gains. As Betts shows so well in many of her short stories, particularly in "The Mother-in-Law," love *does* involve sacrifice; however, for love to survive, the sacrifice must come from more than one person.

Betts pushes the novel beyond the edge of reality with Tamsen Donner. She appears first as a phantom that Luna watches and hears, and then Tamsen appears to Luna "in a perfectly normal dream," sitting beside her "in the Varsity movie theater in downtown Chapel Hill" (*Teeth,* 110). As though anticipating readers' resistance to the raising of ghosts, Betts has Luna insist that illness has taught her to know exactly the moment when reality reaches its edge; furthermore, were her father to hear of these apparitions, she knows he would look at Luna and ask, "Is she really *mine?*" Betts skillfully presents a ghost who roams the earth for a traditional reason—unfinished business: Tamsen Donner wants to know the fate of Hastings, the perpetrator of their fatal "short-cut." Sam, who has often slipped in to see the film about the tragedy, does not find Luna's ghostly experiences strange and wants to know if Tamsen says "whether that last guy killed her" (*Teeth,* 118). But Luna worries about the ghostly visits, fearful that she "is slipping into total schizophrenia," and declares to herself that "if Tamsen ever appeared in the daylight I would head for the nearest emergency room" (*Teeth,* 147). Unlike Luna and Sam, Paul finds the ghostly appearances unlikely, and when Luna insists on a final confrontation with Tamsen, Paul hopes she will not "hang around all night on the mountain giving C.P.R. to the late Tamsen Donner!" (*Teeth,* 306). Betts undergirds the ghostly visits with Paul's doubts and with Luna's own awareness of their strangeness. Yet Luna talks to Tamsen, describes the woman's clothing, and finally relates to her the information that Hastings led a group to South America and died there. In "The Mother-in-Law," Betts has a troubled ghostly spirit return, hovering about the edges of her house to be assured that her handicapped son is being cared for. In *The Sharp Teeth of Love,* Betts writes far more involved scenes of ghostly appearances, which are also essential to the narrative.

The novel has its share of excitement when Sam is kidnapped again, whisked away in a silver Mazda that, just by luck, Luna sees in time. There follows a visit to the police station where, as is so often true, what *really* has happened sounds absurd to strangers. The frantic search for the silver car pays off (the boy somehow drew crescent moons in the dust of the roof as signals), and finally Paul and Luna discover the remote cabin where Sam is held captive. When they divert the kidnappers' attention, Sam bolts and runs out of sight. Now Paul and Luna must hike through rugged terrain to safety, a dangerous undertaking that brings Nancy Finch's Grand Canyon ordeal to mind. Sam is at last found and saved not only from his injuries but also from the subculture creatures who traffic in child pornography and sex.

Perhaps the most important aspect of *The Sharp Teeth of Love* lies in the dire consequences that cruel and evil actions cause. Luna doubtless becomes anorexic and suicidal because she could never please a man as unreasonable as Martin Stone. And Sam has been so victimized that childhood innocence seems a state he never had. A policeman had told Luna that "if you ever have a boy or girl kidnapped and used for shoplifting and porno movies and sex and as much as a year goes by—listen, you don't want that kid back. He's ruint" (*Teeth*, 108). Paul Cowan wonders if Sam, after his abuse and exploitation, will ever be able to "go back and take algebra, much less shop or computers" (*Teeth*, 166). The insidious presence and power of evil in the world has seldom been so apparent in Betts's fiction. When Luna asks Sam to describe his captors, he "twitched his mouth. . . . Then he shrugged. From this I decided that the man who had slashed his hand was somebody nondescript. It did something to me, thinking that evil could not be recognized for itself but stood next to you, buying stamps at the post office" (*Teeth*, 113–14). Two ordinary-looking men driving a silver Mazda down an Arizona highway, a respectable-looking retired major, and a retired Ford dealer (Steven's father) don't *look* capable of setting afoot evil deeds that destroy, but they are. Paul Cowan sees Sam's ordeal in childhood as evidence that however outmoded a concept Original Sin may be in the latter years of the twentieth century, it is, nevertheless, very much alive. It exists "under other names . . . harsh backgrounds and bad social conditions and weak genes and the sins of the fathers were still functioning in the modern world" (*Teeth*, 286). Betts's Calvinism persists.

If Luna Stone is not as appealing a heroine as Nancy Finch, she shares that character's love of reading. Originally an English major, Luna had planned her honors thesis on Kafka, and the grim tale of "The Hunger Artist" obsesses her when she falls ill. During her hospitalization, Luna begins to draw. From early sketches, she improves, teaching herself in great measure, and becomes a talented illustrator of medical and botanical subjects. Her professional reputation is what brought Steven Grier to her door to draw the illustrations for his dissertation. Allusions to writers (Kafka, Merton, Thoreau, Nietzsche, Mann, Aquinas) and to artists and illustrators (Da Vinci, Dürer, Jan Kalkar, Jan Vanderler, August Horn, Albert Bierstadt, Thomas Moran)—as

well as details of Luna's own artwork enrich the text. And Luna's interest in Carl Jung's notion of synchronicity moves throughout the novel,
showing, as Luna tries to explain to Steven, that some things do not
always simply follow cause and effect but instead "just liked to happen
together" (*Teeth,* 54).

Betts's first novel, *Tall Houses in Winter,* was published in 1957, her
sixth, *The Sharp Teeth of Love,* in 1997. During these four decades, she has
worked seriously at developing her skills as a novelist, has moved
steadily into more intricate plots, has avoided repeating herself in those
plots, and has attempted to push the narrative form beyond ordinary
expectations. From that first novel on, Betts has developed characters—
major and minor—that stay with the reader, and in every novel Betts
recounts *interesting* information from how to carve in stone *(The Scarlet
Thread),* to the behavior of retarded adults *(The River to Pickle Beach),* to
the majesty of the Grand Canyon *(Heading West),* to the suffering caused
by anorexia and depression *(The Sharp Teeth of Love).* If these novels do
not meet Betts's highest expectation, they are most certainly serious and
readable books. Each novel is most decidedly—as Betts herself says of
Souls Raised from the Dead—a "better failure" than its predecessor.

Chapter Five
Private Self—Public Life

The public life of Doris Betts as educator, administrator, parent, and concerned citizen is linked to her other life as novelist, short-story writer, essayist, book reviewer, and critic. Even as her primary interest lies in the fiction she produces, she still devotes time and energy to promote public education and community welfare. There *may* be a town in North Carolina where Doris Betts has not spoken at a friends of the library meeting, but there aren't many. The record of her public life is documented in North Carolina newspapers, which report her speeches and appearances. Her concern for people is genuine and reverberates in the lives of her fictional characters.

She served on the school board in Sanford, North Carolina, as her children went through the public schools, on the North Carolina Library Board of Trustees, and on the North Carolina Tercentenary Commission. When North Carolina mandated that every county assess the needs of, and services for, the elderly, Doris Betts headed the Chatham County study, giving her report the title "Tomorrow . . . We'll Be the Old Folks."[1] Her activities are often close to home; sometimes they encompass the entire South.

In 1986 the Honorable William F. Winter, former governor of Mississippi, was chair of the Commission on the Future of the South. The 19-member commission was part of the Southern Growth Policies Board, whose chairman was the Honorable Bill Clinton, governor of Arkansas. The specific goal of the commission, spelled out by then-governor Clinton, was to produce "a short, readable report . . . which can be used . . . to mobilize support for those public policies and public-private partnerships which will increase the per capita income, reduce poverty, and reduce unemployment for Southerners by 1992."[2] The yearlong study, involving 12 southern states, focused on 10 regional objectives to achieve the three-part goal Governor Clinton proposed.

When the commission issued its report, the local paper in Southern Pines, North Carolina, took notice. "It's called 'Halfway Home and a Long Way to Go,' and it may well become one of the most popular publications of the year because the Commission of the Future of the South had the good sense to turn the material it had gathered . . . to Doris Betts to write into a readable report."[3]

Betts takes details from ordinary life to sharpen a point about changing economics in the South: "They [workers not retrained] can read the ripeness of a tomato or the sky's forecast of rain, but not the directions for installing new machinery" (*Halfway*, 7). Literary allusions slip in as if readers were waiting for them: " 'Beauty is our money crop,' says one of the characters of Georgia novelist Flannery O'Connor" (*Halfway*, 25). Readers are *expected* to understand the biblical allusions: "If part of the burden of history," Betts writes, "is a poor underclass now threatening to become permanently mired in poverty, if one of the South's surprises is how a wall of isolation, like Jericho's, has tumbled almost overnight, we must now decide which parts of our past need preserving and which need to be discarded" (*Halfway*, 8–9).

Freed from bureaucratese, the report is alive with direct sentences that often create balance—"Behind each one [of the 10 objectives] is this general premise: unless we all move forward, nobody's going very far." Others use an unexpected image—"But technology can sit in the South, unused, like the zig-zag sewing machine Grandma was afraid to try" (*Halfway*, 10, 21). It's not surprising that "Halfway Home and a Long Way to Go" had a second printing of 20,000 copies.

Betts's accessible prose has come to diverse readers, many of whom may never have heard of her fiction. In 1988, the Florida Department of Agriculture consulted with Betts in preparing a 30-page booklet on the future of forestry in the state. In 1990, Tim Pittman, director of communications in the North Carolina Governor's Office, asked Betts to write a 1,000-word article to focus statewide attention on the problem of functional literacy. Most newspapers in the state carried her article, and expressions of appreciation came from many, including the governor at that time, James G. Martin. (In this same year, Betts wrote "Literacy Is Everybody's Business" with Robert Donnan, director of communications of the Southern Growth Policy Board, "further discussing one of the ten objectives of the Commission on the Future of the South.")[4] In 1992 a reporter on WRAL-TV in Raleigh charged in an editorial that tenured teachers and professors "get a license for lifetime laziness and neglect of students."[5] The chancellor of the University of North Carolina asked Betts to make the response to the reporter's charges, and she did. In 1997 Betts spoke at the inauguration of James B. Hunt, North Carolina's governor.

If Betts envies writers who lead lives of semiseclusion, she herself has never chosen that path. From her teenage years, she has entered into public life with zest. "Very few writers of fiction," Betts's Chapel Hill friend, novelist Lee Smith, observes, "have *public* lives. I mean, nobody wants them. It is very unusual. It makes her unique as far as I'm concerned. I can't think of any other writer of her stature that has such full and meaningful public life. I really cannot."[6]

Betts's activities also take her on the national scene. From 1978 to 1981, Betts served on the Literature Panel of the National Endowment for the Arts (serving as chairman the third year) and was caught in a barrage of criticism directed at the 1979-to-1980 panel because of the poetry manuscripts selected for grants. The April/May 1981 issue of *Coda: Poets and Writers Newsletter* complained that too many grants were awarded to small presses. Individual poets voiced complaints in inflammatory language.[7] (No complaints apparently were lodged against the fiction selections the panel made.) The matter widened when *New York Magazine* commissioned novelist Hilary Masters to write an essay on the controversy. In the end, the magazine declined to publish the essay because the current editor found it "too literary" (Lindberg, 231). However, Masters's piece, "Go Down Dignified: The NEA Writing Fellowships," enjoyed an "underground" circulation, and finally Stanley Lindberg, the editor of the *Georgia Review,* published the essay along with a response to it by David Wilk (director of the NEA Literature Program), essays "more topical and polemic" than the journal ordinarily considered (Lindberg, 230).

Masters charged that "cronyism is commonplace": judges directed fellowships to writers the judges had either edited or published (often in chapbooks with limited printings); there was too much subsidizing of small presses; and Harper and Row authors received "more literary fellowships than any other commercial house."[8] This last charge came in part because, Masters said, two panelists were Harper and Row authors—Doris Betts and Rita Mae Brown (Masters, 240). Masters concluded that "despite noble intentions . . . the Literature Program has been put into jeopardy, if not disrepute, by such connections as reported in this essay" (Masters, 244). He declared that the chairman for 1981 to 1982 would need to see that the list of authors was of "demonstrable literary merits" and not "another pork-barrel constituency . . . ready for the knife" (Masters, 245). That chairman was Doris Betts.

In "A Restrained Response to 'Go Down Dignified,' " David Wilk wrote that Masters's essay was "dangerously balanced on inaccurate

information, unverified facts and hearsay, false assumptions, and the
crude creations of literary politics."⁹ Wilk continued with 24 numbered
responses to Masters's errors.

These two essays provoked so many reactions that the *Georgia Review*
published 13 pages of letter responses, the first of which was from Doris
Betts, who left no doubt about her Piedmont North Carolina heritage.
Because Wilk had commented on many of Masters's errors, Betts said,
she wrote to deal only with Masters's "personal insult" to her.¹⁰ Betts
refuted the charge of partiality to Harper and Row authors: panelists
read manuscripts, not publication affiliations. Furthermore, her connection with Harper and Row had ended in 1973. That said, Betts took on
the more serious matter of ethics. "Perhaps more important, as an elder
in the Presbyterian Church, I will set my Calvinist ethics against his any
day in the week; they are tough-minded enough to permit me also to
take solid Calvinist offense and belt him one next time I see him" (letter
in "Readers' Forum," 897).

Betts agreed to describe the workings of the Literature Panel as well as
"her feelings about three years of reviewing grant applications and setting policies" for *The Culture Post,* published by the National Endowment
of the Arts. She perhaps alludes to the Masters brouhaha when she says
that "the normal paranoia of writers who observe the panel from afar
continues to keep the Literature Panel one of the smallest, least funded,
and least popular in the Endowment."¹¹ Of the 4,000 applicants, the
panel had funds for 300 grants, and Betts shares with 3,700 of the applicants "a history of turned-down manuscripts" ("Confessions," 8). Betts
staunchly defends the panel's work within a fallible system. Even though,
Betts wrote, the panel may give "a few sows' ears delusions of grandeur,
miss some geniuses, fund an occasional charlatan . . . every mistake is an
honest one and whets the appetite for the first Dante who might come
along, somebody unexpected, whether as WASP or an Everything Else,
from Wherever, with an accent I can't drawl. . . . Nobody knows for certain who, or even *if* that Dante is. It's a gamble" ("Confessions," 8). She
closes—in typical Betts fashion—with an encouraging plea to new recip-
ients: "Write something wonderful. . . . If you can become a genius on
$12,500, please advise" ("Confessions," 9).

The Ever-Changing South

In 1991 Converse College convened a conference to address the question
"Will There Be a Distinctive South in the Twenty-First Century?" The

same panelists had participated in an earlier conference, and each had also contributed an essay to *The Future South: A Historical Perspective for the Twenty-First Century,* edited by two Converse College professors.[12] Although the panelists agreed that the South was ever changing, their predictions about its remaining a distinctly different part of the country differed. Shopping malls, television announcers, and lightning-quick communication make the South resemble the rest of the country, but as Betts pointed out, the idea of "southernness" still exists. Many southern writers, when the occasion arises, can play the game: in the company of northerners striking a superior air, a southern drawl is handy. "If you are going to be underestimated by people who speak more rapidly," Betts says, "the temptation is to speak slowly and strategically and outwit them."[13]

Betts herself has lived through decades of a changing South. She grew up when small-town southern life engaged in family dinners on Sunday, a time when relatives finally left the dinner table and ambled "into the woods to get our toothbrushes directly from the trees."[14] In the 1950s, Betts took her young children home to visit, pleased to see them "on the lap of our grandmother, who'll be their great-grandmother, and we'd had again that sense of both time and timelessness which comes from watching one generation blend into the next."[15] When the Chapel Hill campus was distracted in 1969 by demonstrations to improve the lot of the cafeteria workers, some of Betts's students were dismayed when she did not suspend class and join the protest. These young people of the turbulent sixties "could not understand that I believed the cafeteria workers deserved better pay and situation, and when they learned that most of these workers earned more money than I did, they were baffled that I did not lead a picket line. I told them I would honor my teaching contract, that my word was my bond. I told them I did not think this was the way to help the workers, and that they were now being used by groups creating more problems than were solved."[16] In 1972, when the Watergate scandal filled the television screens, Betts remarked that the southern reaction was to say, " 'It's a disgrace,' and to add immediately, 'What else did you expect?' Human perfidy saddens but does not surprise us."[17] It's an insight Betts has long known, as had her grandfather, John Guy Freeze. He "had been taught Original Sin before he was even old enough to be *average* mean, at an age when he had never seen one human being strike another. When I asked him what he thought of Original Sin now that he was sixty-five, he said, 'After all these years, ain't never been disabused' " (1974 address).

The essay Betts contributed to *The Future South,* entitled "Many Souths and Broadening Scale: A Changing Southern Literature," emphasizes the many "sub-souths" that furnish writers subject matter "modified by geography, age, gender, race, and economic class."[18] The look of things in the South has been altered by more than high-rise parking decks and near look-alike fast-food restaurants. Changes have edged the region "closer to national norms than it used to be. The satellite dish stands where the outhouse used to lean; after the tobacco curing barn gave way to the sharecropper's cabin, that was replaced by a rusting trailer, and now by an elaborately furnished mobile home that cost $35,000" ("Many Souths," 178). With similar "airports, malls, hotel chains, fast food restaurants, television programs, most suburbs, highways, billboards, and city outskirts, the drive from New Jersey to Atlanta offers few surprises" ("Many Souths," 178). The "new" southern writers, Betts suggests, will not live in Andalusia on the fringe of Milledgeville, Georgia, as did Flannery O'Connor, or in Covington, Louisiana, as did Walker Percy, or in the hamlet of Pittsboro that Betts calls home. Their writing will more and more reflect the urban and the urbane, as well as the technological and international forces that are no longer kept above the Mason-Dixon line, but are thriving in the Research Triangle Park of North Carolina. "It is a safe prediction," Betts says, "that there will be a broadening of scale" ("Many Souths," 181). Still, Betts conjectures, even though many of these young southern writers may have had more television than book time growing up and are removed from the South of Faulkner, O'Connor, Percy, and Welty, regionalism may survive in their pages. "Perhaps, the regionalism of southern literature will become for readers what it has always aspired to be—a local means to universal ends, not a de facto minor league of letters recognizable by outdated obsessions" ("Many Souths," 184–85).

Betts likes to recall the late Guy Owen, who knew "that the whole story of the human heart could be told on one tobacco farm in eastern North Carolina." Betts declares that the "future of southern literature lies in how well its writers can do the former, not in how accurately they reproduce the latter" ("Many Souths," 185). In her foreword to *New Southern Writing* (1980), Betts found that the stories in the volume did not, in fact, present "new Southern writing." Instead, she found "some good prose by skillful young American writers most of whom have southern origins, jobs, or locations."[19] Indeed, Betts finds the "southern" element in the younger generation of writers has diminished and that now, "like an herb, the southern quality flavors the dish but does not dominate it" ("Foreword," iv). Nevertheless, Betts hopes that these younger writers will tell stories, not propound theses.

Perhaps no place exhibits the current "new South" as dramatically as Atlanta, but in North Carolina, Research Triangle Park, the realized dream of the late governor Luther Hodges, has become "one of the hottest growth areas in the nation."[20] Rising from 6,800 acres of spent tobacco farmland, some 70 companies and 34,000 people have created a "regional image newly minted from red neck to high-tech" (Newman, 126). If tobacco farming has deserted these acres, innovation and research have flourished, producing AstroTurf, bar codes, the cancer drug Taxol, and the AIDS drug AZT. Positioned near North Carolina State University at Raleigh, Duke University at Durham, and the University of North Carolina at Chapel Hill, Research Triangle Park has raised the area's population to 690,000, a figure that may reach 1,000,000 by the year 2000.

Yet there is a curious mingling of the past. An urbane Chapel Hill restaurant offers "Collard greens, topped with shavings of imported Parmesan Cheese" (Newman, 129). A more genuine backward glance is Needmore, a red-clay hamlet of trailers and a few houses, located between Lexington and Statesville near the center of the Piedmont. The few people remaining there grew up on the margin in a hard farming life and today are more attuned to the past than the high-tech present. Cathy Newman balances her *National Geographic* article on Research Triangle Park with a visit to the home of Martha Ward in Needmore, where the tour centered in Martha's pantry. There, aligned for anybody's inspection, are "16 shelves of shoulder-to-shoulder Mason jars. Pears (two kinds), apples (three), pickles (bread-and-butter, sour, dill). And infinitely more, not to mention a Cadillac-long freezer stuffed with meat" (Newman, 118).

Martha Ward has probably never set foot on the grounds of Research Triangle Park, gone through downsizing and outsourcing, or worried about the Dow Jones fluctuations. She grew up on a tenant farm, poor but never on welfare, with a father who "would tie on a sack before he'd accept clothes from anyone" (Newman, 118). Martha Ward inherited his pride and survival skills and can from experience tell the city reporter: "Honey, I've got my emergency cow, and my pantry is full . . . You can't trust them jobs" (Newman, 118).

Newman ends her article about the Piedmont of North Carolina and its impressive high-tech park with Doris Betts, who ruminated not on the industrial and economic changes in the Piedmont but instead on the landscape. "Out east," she says, "we have scrub oaks. . . . They are spindly, useless. No good for lumber or even firewood. We have a saying—they're no good for anything except holding the world together. That's like our people. No good for anything except . . . holding the world together" (Newman, 138). Betts has participated in many activities with colleagues at Research Triangle Park, but in a flash she would honor the survival skills of Martha Ward.

A Writer of the Piedmont

As Betts meets the obligations of a busy public life, she engages in the private endeavor of writing. In her earliest stories, Betts explores themes about love, family life and conflict, loyalty, betrayal, responsibility, and death, and she continues to explore these themes. Among these projects is a new short-story collection, which will surely include her splendid story "This Is the Only Time I'll Tell It."[21] Essays on gardening may also be gathered into a collection, but her energy primarily centers on novels. For some years, Betts has worked off and on with a manuscript tentatively called *Wings of the Morning,* a historical novel that returns for its setting to her fictional Stone County, tracing a family chronicle from 1890 into the 1970s. The central character is Pressley Bostian, an orphan who becomes a Presbyterian minister and patriarch of a large and complicated family. Bostian's life, Betts remarks, "roughly parallels the twentieth century, during which he watches religion lose its power in American life."[22] (Betts soon realized that *Wings of the Morning* was going to be a long book and turned from it to write *Souls Raised from the Dead.*) The manuscript has problems, but Betts plans to finish it even after discovering "to my horror, there has now been another novel published with that title, which is, of course, from the Psalms, and that shook me" (Ketchin, 240). *Wings of the Morning* has been further delayed by *The Sharp Teeth of Love* and more recently by a novel-in-progress called *Who Is Sylvia?*

It will be interesting to see if Betts does indeed return to the fictional locale she created at the beginning of her career.[23] Her shifting the locale of *Heading West* and *The Sharp Teeth of Love* to the West shows Betts's versatility, but she is altogether more at home in the Piedmont of North Carolina. Here her characters belong to the place where they work and live; here the details of house and field, small-town street and front-porch conversations are rendered with a distinctive sense of *place.* Lee Smith likes to recall a comment Betts's student Tim McLaurin made about the importance of place in fiction. "I'll tell you how important it is to me," McLaurin said as he reached into his pocket and dragged out "a rumpled, dusty plastic bag clotted with something dark. 'This is dirt from my family's pasture.' "[24] In *Wings of the Morning,* Betts may choose to return to her "family pasture," once again setting her fiction completely at home.

Betts has influenced many of the younger generation of southern writers, several of whom she has taught and many of whom she has encouraged, particularly through the North Carolina Writers Network. She, however, takes her place as novelist in the company of her fellow contemporaries from the South—Gail Godwin, Anne Tyler, Ellen Gilchrist, Reynolds Price—and in the inherited company of other southerners—Eudora Welty, Peter Taylor, William Faulkner, Flannery O'Connor, and Walker Percy. Betts's writing life, of course, has not been formed entirely by southern influence, but southern writers and, even more important, the people and mores of the Piedmont of North Carolina are the subject matter that she has made her own.

In *Postmortem,* the mystery writer Patricia Cornwall (Daniel) writes a tense scene in which her character Brenda Steppe "was reading Doris Betts, it appeared, before switching off her bedside light that Friday night."[25] And many "real" people are also reading Betts and discovering characters who linger in the mind, a humor that endures, and issues that speak to their concerns. Lee Smith compares Betts's work to that of Marguerite Yourcenar—their "books are really *about* something, they're not only chronicling life—which is fine—but they are really *about* something" (Smith, n.p.). Edification, Betts readily says, "is not the purpose of literature"; on the other hand, she quickly adds, "I am not willing to trivialize its effects either—books have affected me ever since I wanted to be Heidi and go up the mountain and live on bread and cheese."[26]

Throughout the 1995 school year, the second graders in Statesville's Northview Elementary School wrote letters to prominent people, asking about their occupations and their lives. Betts responded with a two-page letter. She told the children about her own second-grade reading experiences with Mrs. Leinster and urged them to pursue reading and writing. She assured these young students that "whatever you learn about writing and words will help you no matter what kind of work you do. . . . Be your best!"[27] It is advice she herself has followed all of her life.

Notes and References

Chapter One

1. Dorothy M. Scura, "Doris Betts at Mid-Career: Her Voice and Her Art," in *Southern Women Writers: The New Generation*, ed. Tonette Bond Inge (Tuscaloosa: University of Alabama Press, 1990), 163.

2. Doris Betts, "Daughters, Southerners, and Daisy," in *The Female Tradition in Southern Literature*, ed. Carol S. Manning (Urbana: University of Illinois Press, 1993), 271; hereafter cited in the text as "Daisy."

3. Library dedication in Chatham (North Carolina) County, address, ts., 28 June 1981, Doris Betts Collection, Mugar Memorial Library, Boston University.

4. "Coincidences and Promises," manuscript speech, 4 June 1981, Doris Betts Collection, Mugar Memorial Library, Boston University; hereafter cited in the text as "Promises."

5. Doris Betts, "BOOKING PASSAGE: Bible Reading," *News and Observer* (Raleigh), 26 June 1994: 5G; hereafter cited as "Reading."

6. Doris Betts, "My Grandfather Haunts This Farm," *Saturday Evening Post*, January–February 1977, 86; hereafter cited in the text as "Grandfather."

7. Doris Betts, "The End of Summer," *Carolina Quarterly* 10 (Spring 1958): 7–16.

8. Anne Tyler, "Stories of Escape and Love in *Beasts of the Southern Wild*," review of *Beasts of the Southern Wild*, by Doris Betts, *National Observer*, week ending 5 January 1974, 15.

9. Susan Ketchin, "Doris Betts: Resting on the Bedrock of Original Sin," in *The Christ-Haunted Landscape: Faith and Doubt in Southern Literature* (Jackson: University of Mississippi Press, 1994), 247; hereafter cited in the text. Elsewhere Betts comments on the foundation-source of Bible stories: "It all went through me, as Charlotte Brontë said once, like wine through water and 'affected the color of my mind.' " George Wolfe, *Kite-Flying and Other Irrational Acts: Conversations with Southern Writers*, ed. John Carr (Baton Rouge: Louisiana State University Press, 1972), 170.

10. W. Dale Brown, "Interview with Doris Betts," *Southern Quarterly* 34, no. 2 (1996): 94; hereafter cited in the text as W. Brown.

11. Doris Betts, "Author Comments on Associate Reformed Presbyterian—Members, History," *Statesville Daily Record*, 8 April 1990, 8C.

12. Elizabeth Evans, "Conversations with Doris Betts," *South Carolina Review* 28, no. 2 (1996): 8; hereafter cited in the text.

13. Jean Ross, "Interview: Doris Betts," in *Contemporary Authors,* New Revision Series, vol. 9, ed. Ann Evory and Linda Metzger (Detroit: Gale, 1983), 54; hereafter cited in the text.

14. Doris Betts, "Teaching Students to Write Creatively," panel discussion, North Carolina English Teachers Association, Summer Conference, Duke University, 1956, Doris Betts Collection, Mugar Memorial Library, Boston University; hereafter cited in the text as "Teaching."

15. Dannye Romine Powell, *Parting the Curtains: Interviews with Southern Writers,* photographs by Jill Krementz (Winston-Salem: John F. Blair, 1994), 16; hereafter cited in the text.

16. While Betts held this part-time job, a young black woman was also employed but relegated to a maid's position. The experience was the germ for Betts's story "Clarissa and the Depths."

17. There had been an earlier publishing success. "I made a whole dollar, and I was going to frame it. It was for a poem that appeared on the inside cover of King Comics, which everybody read back then. . . . that comics prize is the first time I ever made any money from anything. It's having an audience for the first time." Rod Cockshutt, "Q&A with Doris Betts," *Tar Heel: A Magazine of North Carolina* (December 1981): 45.

18. Tony Cacciarelli, ed., "Talk about Writing: Portraits of North Carolina Writers" (Raleigh: North Carolina State University Humanities Extension, 1990), videocassette.

19. Memorandum from Doris Betts to Lettie Teague, n.d., Doris Betts Collection, Mugar Memorial Library, Boston University; hereafter cited as "Memo." Although Lettie Rogers did not have Betts as a student, during the "communist episode," Rogers did invite Betts to coffee and "talk." Rogers published three novels: *The Storm Cloud* (1951), *Landscape of the Heart* (1953), and *Birthright* (1957). She died from cancer at age 39.

20. Doris Betts, letter to Louise Hardeman Abbot, Friday [1955].

21. Rosemary Waldorf, "Out of the Ordinary," *Carolina Alumni Review* (January/February 1995): 28.

22. Doris Betts, "Undergraduate Creative Writing Classes," *ADE Bulletin* 79 (Winter 1984): 34; hereafter cited in the text as *ADE.*

23. Doris Betts, "Realistic Transfer Proposals for Two-Year Institutions," speech, North Carolina Community College Conference, 29 May 1974; hereafter cited in the text as "Proposals."

24. Leonard Rogoff, "Culture and Its Rightful Heirs: Doris Betts on Higher Education," *Spectator,* 30 May–5 June 1985, 5; hereafter cited in the text.

25. Flannery O'Connor, "Fiction Is a Subject with a History—It Should Be Taught That Way," *Collected Works,* ed. Sally Fitzgerald (New York: Library of America, 1988), 850.

26. Guy Friddell, "Today's High Schoolers Can't Write," *Roanoke Times and World News,* 3 April 1977, F1.

27. Doris Betts, "Your Student Writer and Mine," *North Carolina Education* (April 1972): 14; hereafter cited in the text as "Student Writer."

28. "Winstons taste good *like* a cigarette should." Emphasis added.

29. Betts to Staff, "Bottomless Memo," 27 November 1973.

30. Betts to Staff, "Bottomless Memo," 30 August [1974].

31. Betts to Staff, "Bottomless Memo," n.d.

32. William L. Andrews, letter to Doris Betts, 9 March 1994, Doris Betts Collection, Mugar Memorial Library, Boston University.

33. Doris Betts, interview by William Friday, *North Carolina People*, UNC-TV, 1994, videocassette; hereafter cited in the text as *People* video.

34. Robert Hughes, letter to Doris Betts, 30 June 1979, Doris Betts Collection, Mugar Memorial Library, Boston University.

35. Mark William Scandling, "Profiles of Three North Carolina Writers: Doris Betts, Lee Smith, Daphne Athas" (M.A. thesis, University of North Carolina at Chapel Hill, 1979), 13; hereafter cited in the text.

36. Doris Betts, "Many Souths and Broadening Scale: A Changing Southern Literature," in *The Future South: A Historical Perspective for the Twenty-First Century*, ed. Joe P. Dunn and Howard L. Preston (Urbana and Chicago: University of Illinois Press, 1991), 182.

37. Doris Betts, "Keeping All the Options Open: The Christian Vocation in the Secular Academy," *Image: A Journal of the Arts and Religion* 11 (Fall 1995): 72.

38. Evaluation comments (unsigned), Conference on the Teaching of Creative Writing, University of Denver, 1977, Doris Betts Collection, Mugar Memorial Library, Boston University.

39. Doris Betts, letter to Kathleen Scullin, Student Writing Contest, Mount Mary College, Milwaukee, n.d., Doris Betts Collection, Mugar Memorial Library, Boston University.

40. Tim McLaurin has published *Cured by Fire* (New York: G. P. Putnam's Sons, 1995), *Keepers of the Moon* (New York: Norton, 1991), and *Woodrow's Trumpet* (New York: Norton, 1989).

41. Tim McLaurin, "What I Learned from Doris Betts," in *The "Home Truths" of Doris Betts,* with a bibliography, Proceedings of the Eighth Annual Southern Writers Symposium, ed. Sue Laslie Kimball and Lynn Veach Sadler (Fayetteville, N.C.: Methodist College Press, 1992), 29; hereafter cited in the text.

42. Randall Kenan has published *A Visitation of Spirits* (New York: Anchor Books, 1990), *James Baldwin* (New York: Chelsea House, 1994), and *Let the Dead Bury Their Dead and Other Stories* (New York: Harcourt Brace Jovanovich, 1992).

43. Randall Kenan, "Doris Betts: Writer, Teacher, and Rebel," in *The "Home Truths" of Doris Betts,* with a bibliography, Proceedings of the Eighth Annual Southern Writers Symposium, ed. Sue Laslie Kimball and Lynn Veach Sadler (Fayetteville, N.C.: Methodist College Press, 1992), 34.

44. Laura Alderson, "An Interview with Doris Betts," *Poets and Writers* 20 (January/February 1992): 42; hereafter cited in the text.

45. David L. Walker, letter to Doris Betts, 20 March 1995, Doris Betts Collection, Mugar Memorial Library, Boston University.

46. Bill Finger, "Scared and Laughing: Writer Doris Betts at Critical Juncture," *Leader: A Magazine of the Triangle,* 6 April 1989, 17.

47. Joseph M. Flora, interview by Elizabeth Evans, 1 December 1994.

48. Doris Betts, Keynote Address, Katherine Kennedy Carmichael Residence Hall Dedication, ts., 7 November 1989, Doris Betts Collection, Mugar Memorial Library, Boston University; hereafter cited in the text as Keynote Address.

49. Barbara R. Habel [Hyde], letter to Doris Betts, 18 November 1991, Doris Betts Collection, Mugar Memorial Library, Boston University.

50. The position of chairman of the faculty at the University of North Carolina at Chapel Hill, an elected post, is the "most prestigious, influential, and demanding campus position." Rosemary Waldorf, "Out of the Ordinary," *Carolina Alumni Review,* January–February 1995, 26; hereafter cited in the text.

51. Doris Betts, Memorandum to Members of the General Faculty, 12 May 1985.

52. Resolution in Appreciation of Doris W. Betts for Chair of the Faculty, 9 April 1985, Doris Betts Collection, Mugar Memorial Library, Boston University.

53. "Tribute to Doris Betts," *Pembroke Magazine* 18 (1986): 281; hereafter cited in the text as "Tribute."

54. Sarah Cagle and Kristin Hicks, "Education on the Rebound," *Phoenix: Student Newsweekly,* 22 March 1990, 6; hereafter cited in the text.

55. The committee called for real change; for example, Recommendation 14: A coach should be evaluated on several criteria, and his win-loss record shall be only one of the considerations by which his status in this University is determined. Report of the Ad Hoc Committee on Athletics and the University, 15 December 1989, North Carolina Collection, Wilson Library, University of North Carolina at Chapel Hill.

56. James H. Thompson, letter to Doris Betts, 4 August 1972, Doris Betts Collection, Mugar Memorial Library, Boston University.

57. Doris Betts, *Souls Raised from the Dead* (New York: Knopf, 1994), 173.

58. Doris Betts Collection, Mugar Memorial Library, Boston University.

59. Susan Farrington, "Betts Bets on Southern Writers," *Sanford Daily Herald,* 21 March 1992, 2B; hereafter cited in the text.

60. Even though Betts has taught in Chapel Hill for some three decades, she has preferred to live elsewhere.

61. Ken Flora, "South's Literary Surge Linked to Teachers," *Danville (Va.) Register and Bee,* 19 November 1995, 11B.

62. Doris Betts, "Whispering Hope," *Image: A Journal of the Arts and Religion* 7 (Fall 1994): 84; hereafter cited in the text as "Whispering Hope."

63. Lynn Dean Hunter, "A Renaissance Woman," *Virginia-Pilot and the Ledger Star,* 24 July 1944, J3.

64. Doris Betts, memorandum to Rachel Rader and Kate Larkin, 18 March 1995, Doris Betts Collection, Mugar Memorial Library, Boston University.

65. Doris Betts, Installation Sermon, ts., St. Stephen's Episcopal Church, Goldsboro, N.C., 28 December 1993, Doris Betts Collection, Mugar Memorial Library, Boston University; hereafter cited in the text as Sermon.

66. Doris Betts, "Southern Writers and the Bible," in *The Bookmark,* vol. 53 (Chapel Hill: The University Library and Friends of the Library, 1985), 11; hereafter cited in the text as *Bookmark*. Betts may well have illustrated the doctrine of grace by quoting Ephesians 2:8, "For by grace are ye saved through faith; and that not of yourselves: it is the gift of God."

67. Doris Betts, "Faith and Intellect," remarks at Graham Lecture, University of North Carolina at Chapel Hill, 28 September 1982, ts., University of North Carolina at Chapel Hill News Bureau; hereafter cited in the text as "Faith."

68. Doris Betts, "On Religion: Believing Is OK but Keep It Quiet," *Chapel Hill News,* 25 May 1994, A1 ("Village Voices" column).

69. David Marion Holman, "Faith and the Unanswerable Questions: The Fiction of Doris Betts," *Southern Literary Review* 15, no. 1 (1982): 18.

70. Joseph M. Flora, interview by Elizabeth Evans, 1 December 1994.

71. Mary Anne Ferguson, "Southern Women Writers: Beyond the Tradition, The Case of Doris Betts," address, Northeast Modern Language Association, 1979, ts., 2, Doris Betts Collection, Mugar Memorial Library, Boston University; hereafter cited in the text.

72. Doris Betts, letter to Louise Hardeman Abbot, 10 September 1954.

73. Doris Betts, letter to Louise Hardeman Abbot, 25 October 1958.

74. Doris Betts, interview, *Daily Tar Heel* (University of North Carolina at Chapel Hill), 4 November 1995, 5.

75. Joe Knox, "Book Headlines: Doris Betts," *Greensboro Daily News,* 5 October 1975, B1.

76. Anne Marie Riener, "Doris Betts, Part Dreamer, Part Analyst," *SHE* 19 (November 1973): 7; hereafter cited in the text.

77. Harriet Doar, "Three Writers Gauge Feministic Freedom," *Charlotte Observer,* 5 November 1972, 6E.

78. Tim Harrel, "Betts Receives Literary Award," *Daily Tar Heel* (University of North Carolina at Chapel Hill), 18 November 1974, 4.

79. Judy Bolch, "For Writer, Human Heart Is the Biggest Terrain," *Raleigh Times,* 9 February 1981, 1B.

80. Doris Betts, draft letter to Chancellor's Search Committee, University of North Carolina at Chapel Hill, 5 December 1987, Doris Betts Collection, Mugar Memorial Library, Boston University; hereafter cited in text as Search letter.

81. Dannye Romine Powell, "Mettle and Metaphor: N. C. Writer Doris Betts Believes in the Power of Fiction and Feistiness," *Charlotte Observer,* 6 March 1994, F6.

82. Doris Betts, "Home Values in the Fiction of Doris Betts," remarks and reading to the North Carolina–Virginia College English Association, Appalachian State University, Boone, N.C., 7 October 1995.

83. Doris Betts, "Necromancer," *Long View Journal* 1, no. 3 (Winter 1970): 144; hereafter cited in the text as "Necromancer."

84. "Women Writers, Southern Girlhood, and Daisy," ts., 4–5, Doris Betts Collection, Mugar Memorial Library, Boston University.

85. Doris Betts, letter to Louise Hardeman Abbot, Thursday [1954].

86. Jennifer Howard, "Doris Betts," *Publishers Weekly,* 25 April 1994, 43; hereafter cited in the text.

87. Doris Betts, address, Support for the Women's Center at University of North Carolina at Chapel Hill, ts., n.d., Doris Betts Collection, Mugar Memorial Library, Boston University.

88. Doris Betts, introduction to *Southern Women Writers: The New Generation,* ed. Tonette Bond Inge (Tuscaloosa: University of Alabama Press, 1990), 6; hereafter cited in the text as Introduction.

89. Doris Betts, "Notebook No. 1—Basketball," *Sanford Daily Herald,* 15 March 1957, 10.

90. Doris Betts, letter to Louise Hardeman Abbot, [March 1957]. Betts's journalism career includes writing for the *Statesville Daily Record* and the Woman's College News Bureau; ongoing freelance articles for various newspapers including the *Charlotte Observer, Greensboro Daily News,* and *Winston-Salem Journal;* full-time reporter and daily columnist for the *Sanford Daily Herald* (1957–1958); editorial board member for the *North Carolina Democrat* (1958–1960); full-time editor for the Sanford, North Carolina *News Leader* (1960); columnist for the *Chapel Hill News* (1994).

91. Doris Betts, "Hitting the High Spots," *Statesville Daily Record,* 27 October 1949, 4; references to this and subsequent columns are cited by date and page.

92. After Betts began her weekly school column, students in various schools throughout the county began submitting similar columns.

93. As a "sports stringer," Betts called in high school game scores to newspapers in Winston-Salem and Charlotte as well as Greensboro often at 1 A.M. and 2 A.M.

94. Doris Betts, "The Hand That Rocks the Cradle," *Sanford Daily Herald,* 24 April 1957, 10.

95. Doris Betts, "The First 'Good Ole Girl,' " *Life,* March 1980, 126, 128, 130, 132; hereafter cited in the text as *Life* 1980. (At the time, Betts made more money from this article than she had realized from any of her books; response to this article overshadowed news that Betts had just finished a novel.)

96. Doris Betts, "The Agony of the Mothers," *Life,* April 1981, 68–78.

97. Palmer Hill, "Doris Betts Interviews First Lady for Magazine," *Sanford Daily Herald,* 14 February 1980, 16A.

98. Quoted in David Williamson, "Killed for a Penny a Can," *Chapel Hill News,* 5 February 1981, B1.

99. Doris Betts, letter to Scholarship Fund, Medical Foundation, Inc., in memory of James A. Chaney, University of North Carolina at Chapel Hill, 27 June 1993, Doris Betts Collection, Mugar Memorial Library, Boston University.

Chapter Two

1. Peggy Payne, "N.C. Novelist Betts: 'Tired of Being Put in Boxes,' " *News and Observer* (Raleigh), 23 November 1975, 6.

2. Dannye Romine Powell, *Parting the Curtains: Interviews with Southern Writers,* photographs by Jill Krementz (Winston-Salem: John F. Blair, 1994), 21; hereafter cited in the text.

3. "Interview with Doris Betts," *StoryQuarterly* 1 (1975): 71; hereafter cited in the text as *StoryQuarterly.*

4. Doris Betts, letter to Louise Hardeman Abbot, 10 September 1954; hereafter cited in the text as Abbot, letter, 10 September 1954.

5. Doris Betts, letter to Louise Hardeman Abbot, 3 August 1954.

6. Leonard Rogoff, "Culture and Its Rightful Heirs," *Spectator,* 30 May–5 June 1985, 5.

7. Mary Gordon, *Good Boys and Bad Girls* (New York: Viking, 1991), 200.

8. Elizabeth G. Cook, "Iredell Storyteller: Writing Isn't Glamorous, Says Doris Betts," *Salisbury Post* (North Carolina), 13 March 1990, 4A; hereafter cited in the text.

9. Doris Betts, letter to Louise Hardeman Abbot, [November 1954].

10. Quoted in Betty Hodges, "Doris Betts: Writing Is a Series of Choices, of Doing the Worst [?] Over and Over and Over Again," *Durham Morning Herald,* 19 August 1990, F6.

11. Jennifer Howard, "Doris Betts: Conventional 'Southern Themes' Do Not Interest This Writer," *Publishers Weekly,* 25 April 1944, 43.

12. Doris Betts, letter to Louise Hardeman Abbot, [Summer 1954].

13. Margaret Bowen Vanderberry, "The Enigmatic World of Publishing" (honors essay, Department of English, University of North Carolina at Chapel Hill, 1990), 29.

14. Doris Betts, "Literature and the Spiritual Meaning of the Twentieth Century," in *Adventures In Ideas: Lectures and Stories from the Program in the Humanities and Human Values of the College of Arts and Sciences,* ed. Warren A. Nord and Annette Cox (Chapel Hill: University of North Carolina at Chapel Hill, Publications Office of Division of Continuing Education, 1991), 21.

15. A. G. Harmon, "A Conversation with Doris Betts," *Image: A Journal of the Arts and Religion* 11 (Fall 1995): 52; hereafter cited in the text.

16. Doris Betts, "What Has Happened to the Short Story?" address, ts., North Carolina Literary Forum, 12 March 1970, Doris Betts Collection, Mugar Memorial Library, Boston University.

17. Doris Betts, "Brief Prose, Long Subjects," *South Atlantic Quarterly* 72 (1973): 145.

18. Jean Ross, "Interview: Doris Betts," in *Contemporary Authors*, New Revision Series, vol. 9, ed. Ann Evory and Linda Metzger (Detroit: Gale, 1983), 54.

19. George Wolfe, "The Unique Voice, Interview with Doris Betts," in *Kite Flying and Other Irrational Acts: Conversations with Twelve Southern Writers*, ed. John Carr (Baton Rouge: Louisiana State University Press, 1972), 155; hereafter cited in the text. Wolfe published an earlier version of this interview as "An Interview with Doris Betts," *Red Clay Reader* 7 (1970): 12–17.

20. Jan Nordby Gretlund, "An Interview with Eudora Welty," in *Conversations with Eudora Welty*, ed. Peggy Whitman Prenshaw (Jackson: University Press of Mississippi, 1984), 221.

21. Flannery O'Connor, *Mystery and Manners: Occasional Prose*, ed. Sally Fitzgerald and Robert Fitzgerald (New York: Farrar, Straus, and Giroux, 1969), 45.

22. Elizabeth Evans, "Conversations with Doris Betts," *South Carolina Review* 28, no. 2 (1996): 4. Hereafter cited in the text.

23. Michael Kreyling, *Author and Agent: Eudora Welty and Diarmuid Russell* (New York: Farrar, Straus and Giroux, 1991).

24. Jonathan Yardley, "Best Betts Yet," review of *Beasts of the Southern Wild*, by Doris Betts, *Washington Post Book World*, 7 October 1973, 4; hereafter cited in the text as Yardley 1973.

25. Pam Simon, "Doris Betts: Still Learning, Changing, Growing," *Statesville Record and Landmark*, *The Landmark-Leisure Time Magazine*, 9 December 1978, n.p.

26. Doris Betts, "The Fiction of Anne Tyler," *Southern Quarterly* 21, no. 4 (special issue: Contemporary Southern Writers 1) (Summer 1983): 24; hereafter cited in the text as "Fiction."

27. Terry Roberts, "Novelist of Ideas: Doris Betts," *Arts Journal*, July 1984, 10.

28. Laura Alderson, "An Interview with Doris Betts," *Poets and Writers* 20 (January/February 1992): 44.

29. Doris Betts, letter to Louise Hardeman Abbot, [1956].

30. Dorothy M. Scura, "Doris Betts at Mid-Career: Her Voice and Her Art," in *Southern Women Writers: The New Generation*, ed. Tonette Bond Inge (Tuscaloosa: University of Alabama Press, 1990), 162; hereafter cited in the text as Scura 1990.

31. Theodore M. Purdy, letter to Jessie Rehder, n.d., Doris Betts Collection, Mugar Memorial Library, Boston University.

32. J. A. C. Dunn, "Doris Betts at Mid-Passage," *Chapel Hill Weekly*, 3 May 1972, 2.

33. Doris Betts, "Yesterday was the Last Time," *Coraddi* (Woman's College of the University of North Carolina) 56, no. 4 (Summer 1952): 3–5, 10.

34. Robert Tallant, "The Sad People," review of *The Gentle Insurrection and Other Stories*, by Doris Betts, *New York Times Book Review*, 30 May 1954, 4.

35. Evelyn Eaton, "A Fine Debut," review of *The Gentle Insurrection and Other Stories*, by Doris Betts, *Saturday Review*, 10 July 1954, 14.

36. Doris Betts, *The Gentle Insurrection and Other Stories* (New York: G. P. Putnam, 1954), 233–34; hereafter cited in the text as *TGI*.

37. David Marion Holman, "Faith and the Unanswerable Question: The Fiction of Doris Betts," *Southern Literary Journal* 15, no. 1 (Fall 1982): 19.

38. Doris Betts, letter to Louise Hardeman Abbot, [1954].

39. Betts was a sophomore in college when she "received a letter threatening a suit from Thurgood Marshall . . . acting on behalf of the real black people in Statesville upon whom I had based the story. . . . I used one of the person's real names. I never thought about her reading it and being hurt. But she did and she was. . . . We had a personal reconciliation and ultimately the whole business of the suit was dropped." W. Dale Brown, "Interview with Doris Betts," *Southern Quarterly* 34, no. 2 (1996): 103.

40. Robert Penn Warren and Albert Erskine, eds., *A New Southern Harvest: An Anthology* (New York: Bantam, 1957); hereafter cited in the text as *Harvest*.

41. Doris Betts, notes accompanying the manuscript of *The Astronomer and Other Stories*, Doris Betts Collection, Mugar Memorial Library, Boston University; hereafter cited in the text as "Astronomer" Notes.

42. John Lang, "Mapping the Heart's Home: Betts' 'The Astronomer,' " North Carolina/Virginia College English Association, Boone, N.C., 7 October 1995, ts., Doris Betts Collection, Mugar Memorial Library, Boston University; hereafter cited in the text.

43. Doris Betts, *The Astronomer and Other Stories* (New York: Harper and Row, 1966), 30; hereafter cited in the text as *Astronomer*.

44. Mildred Stuart is an early version of Bebe Sellers, the principal character in *The River to Pickle Beach*. Both women fantasize about movies and movie actors who were popular in the 1940s and 1950s.

45. Michael McFee, "Reading a Small History in a Universal Light: Doris Betts, Clyde Edgerton, and the Triumph of Regionalism," *Pembroke Magazine* 23 (1991): 60; hereafter cited in the text. The historic Wallace Brothers herbarium was for decades the largest herbarium in the world. As a youngster, Betts would have passed this building frequently.

46. Clarissa's experience echoes Eudora Welty's "Livvie." Both Clarissa and Livvie deal with old and young men. "Clarissa" first appeared in a 35¢ Bantam edition, "Campus Creative Writing"; Betts earned $25 for the 40-page manuscript.

47. Doris Betts, letter to Louise Hardeman Abbot, 25 October 1958.

48. Benedict Kiely, "The Sky and the River and Man," review of *The Astronomer and Other Stories,* by Doris Betts, *New York Times Book Review,* 6 February 1966, 4.

49. Doris Betts, letter to Louise Hardeman Abbot, [1957].

50. Jonathan Yardley, "About Books," review of *Beasts of the Southern Wild,* by Doris Betts, *Greensboro Daily News,* 7 October 1973, B3.

51. In 1964 Yardley returned to North Carolina from New York and joined the *Greensboro Daily News* as an editorial writer. At that time "the Sunday book-review page . . . had been handled in the 'spare time' of someone on the editorial staff. When the job came open in 1965, Yardley stepped in. At the suggestion of Doris Betts . . . he began a weekly book column and later said, 'I owe almost everything that has happened subsequently to Doris Betts.' " Yardley won a Pulitzer Prize for criticism in 1981 and that same year accepted an offer from the *Washington Post* as book editor. (Linda Brinson, "From the Heart: A Critic Unlocks His Family's Past," review of *Our Kind of People: The Story of an American Family,* by Jonathan Yardley, *Winston-Salem Journal,* 7 May 1989, H12.)
    Yardley praised *Beasts of the Southern Wild* but criticized *Heading West,* calling the concluding portion of the novel "superior women's-magazine fiction."

52. Michael Mewshaw, "Surrealism and Fantasy," review of *Beasts of the Southern Wild,* by Doris Betts, *New York Times Book Review,* 28 October 1973, 41; hereafter cited in the text.

53. Anne Tyler, "Stories of Escape and Love in *Beasts of the Southern Wild,*" review of *Beasts of the Southern Wild,* by Doris Betts, *National Observer,* week ending 5 January 1974, 15; hereafter cited in the text.

54. Doris Grumbach, "Fine Print," review of *Beasts of the Southern Wild,* by Doris Betts, *New Republic,* 10 November 1973, 30.

55. Christopher Brookhouse, "Doris Betts on Writing, Other Writers, the South," *Greensboro Daily News,* 18 November 1973, D3; hereafter cited in the text.

56. Mark William Scandling, "Profiles of Three North Carolina Writers: Doris Betts, Lee Smith, Daphne Athas" (M.A. thesis, University of North Carolina at Chapel Hill, 1979), 9; hereafter cited in the text.

57. *Apostles of Light* by Ellen Douglas was one of the 12 nominations for the National Book Award in fiction. Isaac Bashevis Singer and Thomas Pynchon shared the prize in 1974.

58. "The Glory of His Nostrils" does end "happily" with Wanda Quincey kiting off with a self-declared abortionist who has been "defrocked." But Wanda's bizarre behavior sets her apart from the other women in this collection, who fight their battles in the reality of daily life.

59. Doris Betts, letter to Louise Hardeman Abbot, 25 October 1969.

60. Mary Anne Ferguson, "Beyond the Stereotypes: Southern Women Writers. The Case of Doris Betts," address, Northeast Modern Language Asso-

ciation (1979), ts., Doris Betts Collection, Mugar Memorial Library, Boston University.

61.   Patricia Valenti, "Interview with Doris Betts," WPSO-TV Presents, Pembroke State University Forum, videocassette, 15 February 1989, Doris Betts Collection, Mugar Memorial Library, Boston University.

62.   Betts singled out "Benson Watts Is Dead and in Virginia" because "it's longer, and I always like to do something longer because I figure sooner or later I'm going to learn how to write a novel. And because it provided an excuse for metaphysics." Brookhouse, "Doris Betts on Writing, Other Writers, the South," *Greensboro Daily News,* 18 November 1973, D3.

63.   Doris Betts, *Beasts of the Southern Wild* (New York: Harper and Row, 1973), 154; hereafter cited in the text as *Beasts.*

64.   Warren Leamon, review of *Beasts of the Southern Wild,* by Doris Betts, *South Carolina Review* 7 (1975): 67; hereafter cited in the text. Leamon's discussion of "Benson Watts Is Dead and in Virginia" and "The Spider Gardens of Madagascar" is by far the most insightful consideration to date.

65.   Doris Betts, "The Spell of the Land," readings at North Carolina State University, audiocassette, 16 November 1990, Doris Betts Collection, Mugar Memorial Library, Boston University.

66.   Doris Betts, letter to Howard Gotlieb, 26 May 1969; hereafter cited in the text as Betts 1969.

67.   Doris Betts, "The Ugliest Pilgrim," *Red Clay Reader* 6 (1969): 33–42. The editor, Charleen Whisnant, had already accepted "The Greyhound Minstrel" by Edward Minris but decided to publish both "bus stories" in the same issue. Betts wrote Whisnant that "the bus business couldn't be left out. . . . Maybe you could get Greyhound to buy a thousand copies of RCR this issue and leave one on each bus. . . . How to find love and adventure and leave the driving to us." Doris Betts, letter to Charleen Whisnant, 4 June 1969, Doris Betts Collection, Mugar Memorial Library, Boston University.

68.   The Chamber Theater gave three performances at the University of North Carolina at Chapel Hill in 1980; Michelle Dinsmore adapted a reading there in 1983. "The Spies in the Herb House," "The Mandarin," and "The Ugliest Pilgrim" were presented as one-act plays during a symposium, "The 'Home Truths' of Doris Betts," at Methodist College, Fayetteville, N.C., in 1989.

69.   Betts likes the film "Violet," but finds it, unlike her story, antireligious. Ginnie Lynch, "Theme, Character Transformed from Print to Film," *Phoenix Student Newsweekly,* 13 September 1982, Doris Betts Collection, Mugar Memorial Library, Boston University.

70.   Joe Regal, letter to Doris Betts, 13 September 1995, Doris Betts Collection, Mugar Memorial Library, Boston University.

71.   Doris Betts, postal card to Elizabeth Evans, 13 May 1996.

Chapter Three

1. George Wolfe, "The Unique Voice, Interview with Doris Betts," in *Kite Flying and Other Irrational Acts: Conversations with Twelve Southern Writers*, ed. John Carr (Baton Rouge: Louisiana State University Press, 1972), 162; hereafter cited in the text. This passage also appeared in a 1970 version of this interview published as "An Interview with Doris Betts," *Red Clay Reader* 7 (1970): 15.

2. Doris Betts, letter to Louise Hardeman Abbot, Sunday afternoon [March 1957]; hereafter cited in the text as Abbot, letter, March 1957.

3. Dorothy Scura calls Stone County Betts's Yoknapatawpha. Dorothy Scura, "Doris Betts at Mid-Career: Her Voice and Her Art," in *Southern Women Writers: The New Generation*, ed. Tonette Bond Inge (Tuscaloosa: University of Alabama Press, 1990), 173; hereafter cited in the text as Scura 1990. Betts used the name Stoneville before she found out that there was a real Stoneville in Rockingham County, North Carolina.

4. Borden Deal, "Some Things to Do before Dying," review of *Tall Houses in Winter*, by Doris Betts, *New York Times Book Review*, 3 March 1957, 4; hereafter cited in the text.

5. Doris Betts, *Tall Houses in Winter* (New York: G. P. Putnam's Sons, 1957), 89; hereafter cited in the text as *Houses*.

6. In Anne Tyler's *Breathing Lessons*, Serena's decision to marry Max resembles Jessica's decision to marry Avery. "It's just *time* to marry," Serena said, "that's all. . . . I'm so tired of dating! I'm so tired of keeping up a good front! I want to sit on the couch with a regular, normal husband and watch TV for a thousand years." (Anne Tyler, *Breathing Lessons* [New York: Knopf, 1988], 109.)

7. David L. Stevenson, "Four Views of Love: New Fiction," review of *Tall Houses in Winter*, by Doris Betts, *Nation* (13 April 1957): 329.

8. Sylvia Stallings, "Old Times There Are Not Forgotten," review of *Tall Houses in Winter*, by Doris Betts, *New York Herald Tribune Book Review*, 3 April 1957, 6.

9. Doris Betts, letter to Louise Hardeman Abbot, Thursday [1956]; hereafter cited in the text as Abbot, letter, 1956.

10. William Peden, "Myth, Magic, and a Touch of Madness," review of *The Scarlet Thread*, by Doris Betts, *Saturday Review*, 6 February 1965, 32; hereafter cited in the text.

11. Betts may have found the germ for the strange Miss Bethesda in a news article about Voodoo artist Ida Brown—alias "Dr. Buzzard"—whose powers, like Miss Bethesda's, helped people straighten out love affairs. Shirley Mudge, "Herb Doctor Jailed for Pistol-Totin'," *Sanford Daily Herald*, 5 April 1957, 1.

12. Doris Betts, *The Scarlet Thread* (New York: Harper and Row, 1964), 72; hereafter cited in the text as *Thread*.

13. Doris Betts, "The Novelist's Task: To Keep People from Ending," *Greensboro Daily News*, 18 February 1962, C5.

14. In his will, Bungo Mayfield leaves "my business and anything else I may own to David Allen, because I love him" (*Thread*, 396).

15. Jonathan Yardley, review of *The River to Pickle Beach*, by Doris Betts, *New York Times Book Review*, 21 May 1972, 12; hereafter cited in the text as Yardley 1972.

16. Marjorie M. Bitker, "The People of Pickle Beach," review of *The River to Pickle Beach*, by Doris Betts, *Milwaukee Journal*, 28 May 1972, sec. 5, p. 4; hereafter cited in the text.

17. Jane Plotkin, "Doris Betts: 'Writing Stories Is like Dreaming,' " *Sanford Daily Herald*, 5 December 1974, 2A; hereafter cited in the text.

18. Doris Betts, *The River to Pickle Beach* (New York: Harper and Row, 1972), 70, 72; hereafter cited in the text as *Beach*.

19. "I did see this particular woman and her son—I assumed he was her son. And they did lie in the surf every afternoon. And the affection between them was almost tangible. . . . They moved me very much. . . . And in *Pickle Beach*, too, their 'innocence' and some of the Genesis Cain/McCane associations had value for my themes." Doris Betts, letter to Patrick Morrow, 20 April 1977, Doris Betts Collection, Mugar Memorial Library, Boston University.

Chapter Four

1. Lois Byrd, "They Rode Rafts 225 Miles through Canyon," *Sanford Daily Herald*, 7 August 1971, 16.

2. Dorothy M. Scura, "Doris Betts's Nancy Finch: A Heroine for the 1980s," *Southern Quarterly* 22, no. 1 (Fall 1983): 3; hereafter cited in the text as Scura 1983.

3. Clifton Fadiman, "Heading West," *Book-of-the-Month-Club News*, February 1983, Doris Betts Collection, Mugar Memorial Library, Boston University; hereafter cited in the text.

4. Mary Maguire, letter to Doris Betts, 16 August 1983, Doris Betts Collection, Mugar Memorial Library, Boston University.

5. *3 by 3: Masterpieces of the Southern Gothic*, with an introduction by James P. Simpson (Atlanta: Peachtree Publishers, 1985).

6. Gary Davenport, "The Fugitive Hero in New Southern Fiction," review of *Heading West*, by Doris Betts, *Sewanee Review* 91, no. 3 (Summer 1983): 440–41; hereafter cited in the text.

7. Edmund Fuller, "Three Tales from Tarheel Talents," review of *Heading West*, by Doris Betts, *Wall Street Journal*, 15 December 1981, 30.

8. Review of *Heading West*, by Doris Betts, *Publishers Weekly*, 2 August 1981, 42.

9. Beth Gutcheon, "Willing Victim," review of *Heading West*, by Doris Betts, *New York Times Book Review*, 17 January 1982, 12.

10. Jonathan Yardley, "The Librarian and the Highwayman," review of *Heading West*, by Doris Betts, *Washington Post Book World*, 21 November 1981, 3; hereafter cited in the text as Yardley 1981.

11. Mary Anne Ferguson, "Doris Betts: *Heading West*: A Review Essay," *Southern Quarterly* 21, no. 2 (Winter 1983): 72.

12. Rod Cockshutt, "Q&A with Doris Betts," *Tar Heel: A Magazine of North Carolina*, December 1981, 48.

13. Doris Betts, reading from *Heading West* for "The Spell of the Land," audiocassette, North Carolina State University, 16 November 1990. Betts said of Nancy: "She heads west as a Pharisee; she comes home a Publican."

14. Susan Ketchin, "Doris Betts: Resting on the Bedrock of Original Sin," in *The Christ-Haunted South: Faith and Doubt in Southern Literature* (Jackson: University of Mississippi Press, 1994), 253; hereafter cited in the text.

15. Peggy W. Prenshaw, "Doris Betts's Pilgrims," in *The "Home Truths" of Doris Betts*, with a bibliography, Proceedings of the Eighth Annual Southern Writers Symposium, ed. Sue Laslie Kimball and Lynn Veach Sadler (Fayetteville, N.C.: Methodist College Press, 1992), 83; hereafter cited in the text.

16. A. G. Harmon, "A Conversation with Doris Betts," *Image: A Journal of the Arts and Religion* 11 (Fall 1995): 62.

17. Flannery O'Connor, *Mystery and Manners: Occasional Prose*, ed. Sally Fitzgerald and Robert Fitzgerald (New York: Farrar, Straus, and Giroux, 1969), 113.

18. At one point, Nancy declares that Dwight is "just like Hazel Motes," Flannery O'Connor's character in *Wise Blood*. However, Dwight never experiences the dramatic spiritual crisis that changes the life of Hazel Motes.

19. Doris Betts, *Heading West* (New York: Knopf, 1981), 52; hereafter cited in the text as *West*.

20. Especially effective are Estelle Dover (whose house trailer is stuffed with containers shaped like shoes) and the Grandmother (who "invented her own form of welfare payments. . . . She would carry us boys to sit in different living rooms talking about nothing, smiling . . . not many work any harder for their wages" (*West*, 319).

21. Laura Alderson, "An Interview with Doris Betts," *Poets and Writers* 20 (January/February 1992): 43–44.

22. Publicity material for *Souls Raised from the Dead*, Doris Betts Collection, Mugar Memorial Library, Boston University.

23. Rosellen Brown, "Mary Grace Is Going to Die," review of *Souls Raised from the Dead*, by Doris Betts, *New York Times Book Review*, 17 April 1994, 7; hereafter cited in the text as R. Brown. Barbara Lazear Ascher, "Intensive Caring," review of *Souls Raised from the Dead*, by Doris Betts, *Washington Post Book World*, 15 May 1994, 5; hereafter cited in the text. Robert Wilson, "Kin-

dred 'Souls' Surviving Sorrow," review of *Souls Raised from the Dead*, by Doris Betts, *USA Today*, 29 March 1994, 5D; hereafter cited in the text. Colleen Kelly Warren, "A Family Searches for Signs of Hope," review of *Souls Raised from the Dead*, by Doris Betts, *St. Louis Post-Dispatch*, 17 April 1994, 5C; hereafter cited in the text.

24. Jill Pelaez Baumgaertner, "Suffer the Little Children," review of *Souls Raised from the Dead*, by Doris Betts, *Christian Century*, 12 October 1993, 927; hereafter cited in the text.

25. Doris Betts, "The Courage to Kill," telephone interview by Jon Elsen, *New York Times Book Review*, 17 April 1994, 7.

26. This address "has been reprinted more than anything I ever wrote. Isn't that bizarre?" W. Dale Brown, "Interview with Doris Betts," *Southern Quarterly* 34, no. 2 (1996): 92.

27. Anne Mallard Davis, "Booking on Betts," *Chapel Hill News*, 1 May 1994, A1.

28. Doris Betts, "Whispering Hope," *Image: A Journal of the Arts and Religion* 7 (Fall 1994): 80; hereafter cited in the text.

29. Blake Dickinson, "Chicken Truck Wreck Spurred Idea for UNC Professor's Latest Novel," *Durham Herald Sun* (*Chapel Hill Herald* section), 7 June 1994, 3.

30. Doris Betts, "Anne Holmes Hubbard Memorial Lecture," North Carolina Medical Society Auxiliary, Winston-Salem, 4 May 1993, ts., Doris Betts Collection, Mugar Memorial Library, Boston University.

31. Betts includes lines from "With Her" in the frontispiece of the novel.

32. Cathy Bost, "Statesville Native Gets to Know Those 'Ordinary People' She Writes About," *Winston-Salem Journal*, 24 March 1995, B9; hereafter cited in the text.

33. Notes for *Souls Raised from the Dead*, Doris Betts Collection, Mugar Memorial Library, Boston University; hereafter cited in the text as "Notes." Dr. Blythe took Betts through a dialysis center in Carrboro.

34. At a reading before *Souls Raised from the Dead* was completed, Betts told the audience she welcomed suggestions for a title. A note from Judy Dorminey provided what was needed: "There was a window in an old part of Atlanta now cleared by urban renewal which said, coincidentally,

> KEYS MADE
> KNIVES SHARPENED
> PALMS READ
> SOULS RAISED FROM THE DEAD

35. Doris Betts, *Souls Raised from the Dead* (New York: Knopf, 1994), 133–34; hereafter cited in the text as *Souls*.

36. *The Letters of Francis Thompson,* ed. John Evangelist Walsh (New York: Hawthorn Books, 1969), 69.

37. "Betts Is Back . . . in Stellar Style. The Raising of Reason," *Sanford Daily Herald,* 13 April 1994, 14A; hereafter cited in the text as "Reason." Two other highway patrolmen appear in the plot—one a good, but overeager, born-again Christian; the other an unsavory officer who tears up traffic tickets in return for sex.

38. James Ashton Devereux, S.J., letter to Doris Betts, 1 November 1994, Doris Betts Collection, Mugar Memorial Library, Boston University.

39. At this writing *The Sharp Teeth of Love* had not been published; the novel appeared in spring 1997. All quotations and page numbers in the text, however, refer *not* to the manuscript but to the published version, hereafter cited as *Teeth.*

40. Joe Regal, letter to Doris Betts, 10 August 1995, Doris Betts Collection, Mugar Memorial Library, Boston University.

41. Betts dedicates *The Sharp Teeth of Love* to Joseph M. Flora, whose "invitation to speak to the Western Literature Association in Reno, that Sierra Nevada landscape and especially Donner Pass, were the cause of this story."

42. Doris Betts, remarks and reading, "Home Values in the Fiction of Doris Betts," North Carolina–Virginia College English Association, Boone, N.C., 7 October 1995; hereafter cited in the text as "Remarks."

Chapter Five

1. Dwight Martin, "Novelist Doris Betts Urges Concern for Elder Citizens," *Durham Herald,* 27 August 1990, 6.

2. Doris Betts, *Halfway Home and a Long Way to Go,* report of the 1986 Commission on the Future of the South, Southern Growth Policies Board, 1986, 4; hereafter cited in the text as *Halfway.*

3. *The Pilot* (Southern Pines, North Carolina), 25 November 1986; newspaper clippings, North Carolina Collection, Wilson Library, University of North Carolina at Chapel Hill.

4. Doris Betts and Robert Donnan, *Literacy Is Everybody's Business: The Power of the Word,* The Report on Southern Regional Literacy Commission, Southern Growth Policies Board, Research Triangle Park, N.C., 1990.

5. Doris Betts, response to WRAL-TV editorial (Raleigh), ts., 12 January 1992, Doris Betts Collection, Mugar Memorial Library, Boston University.

6. Lee Smith, interview by Elizabeth Evans, 29 November 1994; hereafter cited in the text.

7. Quoted in Stanley W. Lindberg, "To Our Readers," *Georgia Review* 35 (Summer 1981): 230; hereafter cited in the text.

8. Hilary Masters, "Go Down Dignified: The NEA Writing Fellowships," *Georgia Review* 35, no. 2 (1981): 240; hereafter cited in the text.

9. David Wilk, "A Restrained Response to 'Go Down Dignified,'" *Georgia Review* 35, no. 2 (1981): 246.

10. Doris Betts, letter in "Readers' Forum," *Georgia Review* 35, no. 4 (1981): 897; hereafter cited in the text.

11. Doris Betts, "Confessions of a Literature Panelist," *The Culture Post* (National Endowment of the Arts) 6 (March/August 1981): 9.

12. *The Future South: A Historical Perspective for the Twenty-First Century,* ed. Joe P. Dunn and Howard L. Preston (Urbana: University of Illinois Press, 1991).

13. Doris Betts, conference panel discussion, "Will There Be a Distinctive South in the Twenty-First Century?" videocassette, Converse College, Spartanburg, S.C., 4 May 1991.

14. Doris Betts, "Poet Frost, Yes," *Sanford Daily Herald,* 20 March 1957, 8.

15. Doris Betts, "You Can Go Home Again," *Sanford Daily Herald,* 20 May 1957, 8.

16. Doris Betts, address, ts., Sanford Rotary Club (1969), Doris Betts Collection, Mugar Memorial Library, Boston University.

17. Doris Betts, address, ts., Newspaper Editors Association, Atlanta, Ga., 17–19 April 1974, Doris Betts Collection, Mugar Memorial Library, Boston University; hereafter cited in the text as 1974 address.

18. Doris Betts, "Many Souths and Broadening Scale: A Changing Southern Literature," *The Future South: A Historical Perspective for the Twenty-First Century* (Urbana: University of Illinois Press, 1991), 175. Originally entitled "American Writers from Many Souths."

19. Doris Betts, "Forward" [*sic*], in *New Southern Writing,* edited by Moira Crone (Baltimore: Numen, 1980), v; hereafter cited in the text as "Foreword."

20. Cathy Newman, "North Carolina's Piedmont," *National Geographic* 187, no. 2 (March 1995): 126; hereafter cited in the text.

21. Doris Betts, "This Is the Only Time I'll Tell It," *New Orleans Review* 5, no. 3 (1977): 195–97. Along with remarks, "Prefatory to a Story," this story was reprinted in *Man in Seven Modes,* Proceedings of the Southern Humanities Conference, Winston-Salem, 1977, 32–39. It also appears in *The Rough Road Home: Stories by North Carolina Writers,* ed. Robert Gingher (Chapel Hill: University of North Carolina Press, 1992), 27–34.

22. Susan Ketchin, "Doris Betts: Resting on the Bedrock of Original Sin," in *The Christ-Haunted Landscape: Faith and Doubt in Southern Literature* (Jackson: University of Mississippi Press, 1994), 240–41; hereafter cited in the text.

23. Betts alluded in 1995 to her "new novel" about an embezzler. Doris Betts, remarks and reading, "Home Values in the Fiction of Doris Betts," North Carolina–Virginia College English Association, Boone, N.C., 7 October 1995.

24. Clifton Daniel, "North Carolina's Literary Legacy," *Star-News* (Wilmington), 14 April 1996, 6D.

25. Patricia Cornwall (Daniel), *Postmortem* (New York: Avon Books, 1990), 149.

26. Doris Betts, "Literature and the Spiritual Meaning of the Twentieth Century," in *Adventures in Ideas: Lectures and Stories from the Program in the Humanities and Human Values of the College of Arts and Sciences,* ed. Warren A. Nord and Annette Cox (Chapel Hill: University of North Carolina, Publications Office of the Division of Continuing Education, 1991), 22.

27. "Betts Writes to Local Students," *Statesville Daily Record,* 4 April 1995, B1.

Selected Bibliography

PRIMARY WORKS

Novels

Tall Houses in Winter. New York: G. P. Putnam's, 1957; London: Cassell, 1959; Milan: Rizzoli, 1959; New York: Curtis, 1973.

The Scarlet Thread. New York: Harper and Row, 1964; New York: Curtis, 1973. (Copyright date in the front matter indicates publication in 1964; however, on the dust jacket, 0165 indicates that publication was delayed until January 1965.)

The River to Pickle Beach. New York: Harper and Row, 1972; New York: Curtis, 1973; New York: Scribner Paperback Fiction, 1995.

Heading West. New York: Knopf, 1981; New York: Signet American Library, 1982; New York: Scribner Paperback Fiction, 1995.

Souls Raised from the Dead. New York: Knopf, 1994; New York: Scribner Paperback Fiction, 1995.

The Sharp Teeth of Love. New York: Knopf, 1997.

Short Stories

The Gentle Insurrection and Other Stories. New York: G. P. Putnam's, 1954; London: Gollancz, 1955.

The Astronomer and Other Stories. New York: Harper and Row, 1965; Baton Rouge: Louisiana State University Press, 1996.

Beasts of the Southern Wild and Other Stories. New York: Harper and Row, 1973; Atlanta: Peachtree Publishers, 1985.

Selected Critical Articles

"The Arts in Red and Gold." In *Nine from North Carolina: An Exhibition of Women Artists*, 8–10. Washington, D.C.: National Museum of Women in the Arts, 1989.

"Brief Prose, Long Subjects." *South Atlantic Quarterly* 72 (1965): 283–95.

"Confessions of a Literature Panelist." *The Culture Post* 6 (March–August 1981): 6–9.

"Daughters, Southerners, and Daisy." In *The Female Tradition in Southern Literature,* edited by Carol S. Manning, 259–76. Urbana: University of Illinois Press, 1993.

"The Fiction of Anne Tyler." *Southern Quarterly* 21, no. 4 (1983): 23–37. A special issue on contemporary southern writers.

"The Fingerprints of Style." In *Voicelust: Eight Contemporary Fiction Writers on Style,* edited by Allen Wier and Don Hendrie Jr., 7–22. Lincoln: University of Nebraska Press, 1985. (First published in *Black Warrior Review* 10, no.1 [1983]: 171–84.)

"Forward" [*sic*]. In *New Southern Writing,* edited by Moira Crone, i–v. Baltimore: Numen, 1980.

"The House by the River: Ovid Williams Pierce." *South Atlantic Quarterly* 64 (1965): 283–95.

Introduction to *Southern Women Writers: The New Generation,* edited by Tonette Bond Inge, 1–8. Tuscaloosa: University of Alabama Press, 1990.

"Keeping All the Options Open: The Christian Vocation in the Secular Academy." *Image: A Journal of the Arts and Religion* 11 (1995): 69–73.

"Many Souths and Broadening Scale: A Changing Southern Literature." In *The Future South: A Historical Perspective for the Twenty-First Century,* edited by Joe P. Dunn and Howard L. Preston, 158–87. Urbana: University of Illinois Press, 1991.

"Tyler's Marriages of Opposites." In *The Fiction of Anne Tyler,* edited by C. Ralph Stephens, 1–15. Jackson: University Press of Mississippi, 1990.

"Undergraduate Creative Writing Courses." *ADE Bulletin* 79 (Winter 1984): 34–36.

"Whispering Hope." *Image: A Journal of the Arts and Religion* 7 (Fall 1994): 80–84.

Selected Miscellaneous Publications

"Boiling the Wolf." *North Carolina Education* 4, no. 8 (1974): 12–14.

"Doing Lunch." *New Harmony Journal* 2, no. 1 (28 August 1995): 1–2.

"Fiction Induction and Deduction." *Arts in Society* 2, no. 1 (Summer–Fall 1974): 276–84.

"The First 'Good Ole Girl.' " *Life,* March 1990, 126–32.

"My Grandfather Haunts This Farm." *Saturday Evening Post,* January–February 1977, 62, 85–86.

Literacy Is Everybody's Business. The Power of the Word, with Robert Donnan. Report of the Southern Regional Literacy Commission, Southern Growth Policy Board. Research Triangle Park, n.d.

"Slow-Change Artist" ["Faith and Intellect" address]. *HIS: Monthly Magazine for the College Christian* 43, no. 7 (1983): 4–6.

Turning Over a New Leaf: People and Trees Together, edited by Doris Betts. Tallahassee: Florida Department of Agriculture and Consumer Service Division of Forestry, March 1989.

SECONDARY WORKS

Bibliographies

Kimball, Sue Laslie, and Lynn Veach Sadler, eds. *The "Home Truths" of Doris Betts.* With a bibliography. Proceedings of the Eighth Annual Southern

Writers Symposium. Fayetteville, N.C.: Methodist College Press, 1992. The only extensive bibliography to date, this one is helpful but sometimes inaccurate or incomplete.

Scura, Dorothy M. "Doris Betts." In *Fifty Southern Writers after 1900: A Bio-Bibliographical Source Book,* edited by Joseph M. Flora and Robert Bain, 53–63. New York: Greenwood Press, 1987. Helpful listing of studies about Betts, major newspaper reviews.

Criticism and Interviews

Alderson, Laura. "An Interview with Doris Betts." *Poets and Writers* 20, no. 1 (1992): 36–44. Describes life at Araby Farm and Chapel Hill–Carrboro distinctions; discusses agents and writing students. Comments on *Heading West* and its reviewers.

Brown, W. Dale. "Interview with Doris Betts." *Southern Quarterly* 34, no. 2 (1996): 91–104. Comments on her "Faith and Intellect" address, asserts that many writers are suspicious of deconstruction, and discusses the importance of religion in her background and fiction. Recounts the near lawsuit over "The Sympathetic Visitor" and comments on *Souls Raised from the Dead.*

Cockshutt, Rod. "Q&A with Doris Betts." *Tar Heel: A Magazine of North Carolina* (December 1981): 44–49. Has useful biographical details and especially important comments by Betts on her work as journalist, on *Heading West,* and on the women's movement.

Coleman, John C. "*The Scarlet Thread.*" In *Survey of Contemporary Literature,* edited by Frank N. Magill, 6647–49. Rev. ed. Englewood Cliffs, N.J.: Salem, 1977. Argues that Betts is "not at ease" in the novel form. Finds her descriptions "vivid, sharp, memorable" and sees her major theme, the lack of communication and understanding, as the aspect that gives her short stories their distinction.

Evans, Elizabeth. "Negro Characters in the Fiction of Doris Betts." *Critique* 17, no. 2 (1975): 59–76. Notes the sensitive portrayal of African-American characters in situations where mild or explosive confrontations result. Often stereotyped by occupation, these characters are nevertheless "distinguished by personality and individualized by special traits."

———. "The Mandarin and the Lady: Doris Betts's Debt to Amy Lowell." *Notes on Contemporary Literature* 6, no. 4 (1976): 2–5. Betts acknowledges Lowell's "Patterns" as a source for "The Mandarin" and follows her widowed protagonist into an old age that remains "patterned."

———. "Another Mule in the Yard: Doris Betts's Durable Humor." *Notes on Contemporary Literature* 11, no. 2 (1981): 5–6. Points out the sardonic humor in this backwoods tale.

———. Conversations with Doris Betts." *South Carolina Review* 28, no. 2 (1996): 4–8.

Ferguson, Mary Anne. "Doris Betts." In *American Women Writers,* edited by Lina Mainiero, 151–52. New York: Ungar, 1979. Furnishes a brief biographical survey. Ferguson argues that Betts achieves a "rare authority" in writing about women's experiences. Regrets that Betts has "yielded to writing novels" rather than staying with the short story, where "she succeeds in catching whole lives quickly."

―――. "Doris Betts, *Heading West*: A Review Essay." *Southern Quarterly* 21, no. 2 (1983): 68–76. Sees *Heading West* in the tradition of quest novels. Finds Betts has contributed more toward the understanding of the lower middle class—their attributes, the tragedies of their lives, their longing for meaning—than any other contemporary writer. Criticizes Nancy's marriage as a weak ending—"an alternative, not an escape."

Harmon, A. G. "A Conversation with Doris Betts." *Image: A Journal of the Arts and Religion* 11 (1995): 51–68. Betts maintains strong religious convictions but is not "a didactic writer." Comments on her interest in Pascal, C. S. Lewis, Walker Percy, and Flannery O'Connor. Betts's comments on "The Astronomer," *Heading West,* and *Souls Raised from the Dead* are valuable.

Holman, David Marion. "Faith and the Unanswerable Questions: The Fiction of Doris Betts." *Southern Literary Journal* 15, no. 1 (1982): 15–23. Even though Flannery O'Connor and Betts share "questions, mysteries of faith and iniquity," Holman finds Betts's fictional world "more modern, more complexly confused." When her protagonists venture into the world of experience, they "must finally return home to test the knowledge they have gained."

Howard, Jennifer. "Doris Betts." *Publishers Weekly,* 25 April 1994, 42–43. Discusses Betts's most recent novels as well as her shunning "southern" themes. Has useful facts about Betts's life and teaching at the University of North Carolina.

"Interview with Doris Betts." *StoryQuarterly* 1 (1975): 67–72. Betts comments on her early work, writing habits, influences, and teaching.

Jones, A. Wesley. "*Beasts of the Southern Wild.*" In *Survey of Contemporary Literature,* edited by Frank N. Magill, 579–83. Rev. ed. Englewood Cliffs, N.J.: Salem, 1977. Makes excellent connections of themes among the stories, especially regarding women characters and their relationships. Oddly, Jones does not mention Betts's intriguing "Benson Watts is Dead and in Virginia," the long story that ends this collection.

Ketchin, Susan. "Doris Betts: Resting on the Bedrock of Original Sin." In *The Christ-Haunted Landscape: Faith and Doubt in Southern Literature,* 230–59. Jackson: University Press of Mississippi, 1994. This interview provides the most detailed discussion of Betts's religious background and its influence on her fiction. Has particularly valuable comments on *Souls Raised from the Dead,* on feminism, and on women writers.

Kimball, Sue Laslie, and Lynn Veach Sadler, eds. *The "Home Truths" of Doris Betts.* With a bibliography. Proceedings of the Eighth Annual Southern

Writers Symposium. Fayetteville, N.C.: Methodist College Press, 1992. Includes articles by Betts's students Tim McLaurin and Randall Kenan. Excellent critical essays by Peggy Whitman Prenshaw, Charlotte S. McClure, and Julian Mason, as well as Betts's symposium address.

Madden, David. "*The Astronomer and Other Stories.*" In *Survey of Contemporary Literature,* edited by Frank N. Magill, 418–23. Rev. ed. Englewood Cliffs, N.J.: Salem, 1977. By far the best commentary to date on this collection. Madden finds that the protagonist in each story (usually his or her own antagonist) "utters a characteristic cry at that moment when the reflection of his marooned self in the foreign object which he wills into his constellation, or observes from afar is sharpest." The most poignant example occurs when "the astronomer," Horton Beam, cries to the stars, "Listen! Say something to me!" Madden sees Betts continuing Sherwood Anderson's rendering of the American dream in "Careful, Sharp Eggs Underfoot" by mingling the pathos and grotesque humor of small-town life. These stories, Madden declares, "are all good, the novella ("The Astronomer") is unmistakably brilliant."

McFee, Michael. "Reading a Small History in a Universal Light: Doris Betts, Clyde Edgerton, and the Triumph of True Regionalism." *Pembroke Magazine* 23 (1991): 59–67. Excellent discussion of "The Spies in the Herb House" on three levels: as autobiography, as a child's fall from innocence to experience, and as a regional study of mill town life.

Moose, Ruth. "Superstition in Doris Betts's New Novel." *North Carolina Folklore Journal* 21 (1973): 61–62. Brief discussion of how folklore and superstitions enrich *The River to Pickle Beach*.

Powell, Dannye Romine. *Parting the Curtains: Interviews with Southern Writers.* Photographs by Jill Krementz, 15–31. Winston-Salem: John F. Blair, 1994. Betts recounts life in Statesville and in the Associate Reformed Presbyterian Church as her primary influences. Comments on life as student, teacher, and writer. Notes the religious aspects in *Souls Raised from the Dead* and repeats her belief that cheerfulness, not happiness, should be the pursuit of adults.

Prenshaw, Peggy Whitman. "A Conversation with Seven Fiction Writers." *Southern Quarterly* 29, no. 2 (1991): 69–94. Transcript of a 1989 roundtable with Betts and six other women writers in North Carolina, all of whom give biographical details that affect their writing and discuss their writing and teaching routines. Has a particularly interesting discussion on whether a sense of "southern" exists that can be recognized in current writing.

Ragan, Sam. "Tribute to Doris Betts." *Pembroke Magazine* 18 (1986): 275–84. Notes the progress of Betts's career and her many honors, particularly those from North Carolina.

Ray, William E. "Doris Betts and the Art and Teaching of Writing." In *Man in 7 Modes,* 40–51. Winston-Salem: Southern Humanities Conference Proceedings, 1977. In this excellent interview, Betts discusses the short-story form, the current difficulty of teaching Faulkner to undergraduates, and her responses to Walker Percy, Carson McCullers, Robert Penn Warren, and Reynolds Price. Betts cites her reading preferences in fiction, tells the ideas that led to "The Ugliest Pilgrim," and discusses her view of teaching creative writing.

Reynolds, John R., Stephen Harrison, and Walter Quade. "Doris Betts." *The Rebel* [East Carolina University] (1969): 9–12. One of the earliest published interviews with Betts. At this time, Betts considers herself a short-story writer exclusively. She overstates her adverse reactions to Henry James and Edith Wharton.

Rogoff, Leonard. "Culture and Its Rightful Heirs: Doris Betts on Higher Education." *Spectator,* 30 May–5 June 1985, 5–8. Betts comments on her role at the University of North Carolina, on curriculum matters after William Bennett's mid-1980s pronouncements, and on the purpose of education.

Ross, Jean. "Interview: Doris Betts." In *Contemporary Authors.* New Revision Series, vol. 9, edited by Ann Evory and Linda Metzger, 51–55. Detroit: Gale, 1983. Contains valuable information on Betts's early life, school years, and early stories. Has useful comments on the background for *Heading West* and on the endings of that novel and of "The Astronomer." Betts notes that she had not read Flannery O'Connor when reviewers first compared the two. (Ross has an earlier interview in *Dictionary of Literary Biography Yearbook: 1982,* edited by Richard Ziegfield, 219–27. Detroit: Gale, 1983.)

Scandling, Mark William. "Profiles of Three North Carolina Writers: Doris Betts, Lee Smith, Daphne Athas." M.A. thesis, University of North Carolina at Chapel Hill, 1979. Especially valuable because of interview responses from Betts's teachers (including Frances Gray Patton, Peter Taylor, and C. Hugh Holman) and family members.

———. "Doris Betts: Making a Difference in Many Lives." *Carolina Quarterly* 32, no. 2 (1980): 101–8. Has useful biographical information.

Scura, Dorothy M. "Doris Betts's Nancy Finch: A Heroine for the 1980s." *Southern Quarterly* 22, no. 1 (1983): 3–12. Scura overstates that Nancy Finch "joins, but surpasses, the great female protagonists of American fiction," but her analysis of *Heading West,* particularly of individual characters, is excellent. Notes the rich comic sense, the abundant literary allusions, and the ability or inability of characters to see what is before them. Reprint in *Women Writers of the Contemporary South,* edited by Peggy Whitman Prenshaw, 135–45. Jackson: University Press of Mississippi, 1984.

———. "Doris Betts." In *Fifty Southern Writers after 1900: A Bio-Bibliographical Source Book,* edited by Joseph M. Flora and Robert Bain, 53–63. New York: Greenwood Press, 1987. Has useful biographical and professional facts. Sees the main themes as the treatment of children and old people (often facing death), love in all its manifestations, and the failure to communicate. Scura's commentary on Betts's short stories and novels is helpful and forms the basis for her later article (1990), "Doris Betts at Mid-Career: Her Voice and Her Art." Has a useful bibliography.

————. "Doris Betts at Mid-Career: Her Voice and Her Art." In *Southern Women Writers: The New Generation*, edited by Tonette Bond Inge, 161–79. Tuscaloosa: University of Alabama Press, 1990. Beginning with a helpful biographical discussion, Scura notes Betts's consistent themes, "time and mortality," and sees in the most recent work an emphasis on "earthly love" and on religious experience. Helpful critical commentary follows on the three short-story collections and on the novels.

Walsh, William J. *Speak So I Shall Know Thee: Interviews with Southern Writers.* 40–51. Asheboro, North Carolina: Down Home Press, 1993. In this interview, conducted in 1988, Betts discusses the notion that all writers are regional writers. Makes interesting observations about the changes of student writing and of southern women writers in a postfeminist era. Especially useful for Betts's comments on the comic aspect of her fiction. Includes important biographical anecdotes from Betts's childhood.

Wolfe, George. "The Unique Voice: Doris Betts." In *Kite-Flying and Other Irrational Acts. Conversations with Twelve Southern Writers*, edited by John Carr, 149–73. Baton Rouge: Louisiana State University Press, 1972. Betts comments on early childhood experiences, her involvement in public life, and on her work, particularly "The Astronomer," *The Scarlet Thread,* and "Benson Watts Is Dead and Living in Virginia." (Wolfe's interview appeared earlier in substantially the same form as "Interview with Doris Betts," *Red Clay Reade*r 7 [1970]: 12–17.)

Index

Abbot, Louise Hardeman, 13, 28, 32, 38, 51
American Academy and Institute of Arts and Letters, 23
Arnow, Harriette, "A Problem of Logistics," 48

Barth, John, 40
Baumgaertner, Jill Pelaez, 86, 92
Betts, Doris: and Associate Reformed Presbyterian Church, 2, 4–5; and athletic controversy at UNC, 20–21; biblical stories' influence on, 3, 4; Calvin and Calvinism, 5–6, 10, 40, 102; chair of faculty at UNC, 20; on changing South, 102–6; Chekov's influence on, 40; college years, 11–13; creative writing at UNC, 16–18; early education, 9–10; early life, 6–9; on feminist issues, 28–33, 81–82; focus on novel writing, 42–43; freshman composition program at UNC, 14–16; high school years, 1, 10, 33–35; hometown, 6–8, 51, 60; as journalist, 33–36; major themes, 43–44; male writers' influence on, 41; National Endowment for the Arts, Literature Panel, 101–2; public life, 99–102; recognition at UNC, 21–23, 29, 30–31; reissue of titles, 79–80; religion in fiction, 24–25, 27–28, 40, 51–53, 68–69; religious participation of, 25–26 (see also *Souls Raised from the Dead*); travel, 41–42; on women's friendships, 32; work in progress at UNC, 106

NONFICTION
"Daughters, Southerners, and Daisy" (essay), 32
"Faith and Intellect" (speech), 26, 86
"Halfway Home and a Long Way to Go" (report), 99–100
"Many Souths and Broadening Scale: A Changing Southern Literature" (essay), 104

"My Grandfather Haunts This Farm" (article), 29
"Your Student Writer and Mine" (article), 15

·NOVELS
Heading West, 4, 22, 38, 41, 42, 48, 53, 61, 77, 78–85, 98, 106; *Stepping Westward* (early title), 39; allusions, 80; aspects of evil, 78–79, 83, 84, 85; editorial problems, 39; Grand Canyon, 41, 78, 79, 80, 83, 85, 97, 98; humor, 84; minor characters, 122n. 20; response of reviewers, 81; women's magazine-fiction, 81–82, 85
River to Pickle Beach, The, 8, 61, 70–77, 78, 80, 98, 121n. 19; aspects of evil, 76–77; changing South, 73; characters from *The Scarlet Thread,* 74; epigraphs, 72; minor characters, 76; movies, 8, 72, 75; national tragedies, 70, 71; race relations, 73, 76; sensational elements, 70, 72, 73; television, 71–72
Scarlet Thread, The, 4, 5, 13, 49, 61, 65–70, 77, 78, 98; early titles, 65; minor characters, 67–68; race relations, 66; role of women, 68–70; sensational elements, 66, 120n. 11; social history, 13, 66
Sharp Teeth of Love, The, 5, 31, 38, 41, 42, 53, 57, 77, 93–98, 106; allusions 97–98; anorexia, 95, 97; aspects of evil, 97; Donner Party, 31, 57, 93–94, 96; ghost of Tamsen Donner 57, 95 96; western setting, 93
Souls Raised from the Dead, 4, 5, 11, 22, 23, 25, 26, 37, 42, 44, 57, 79, 84, 85–93, 94, 95, 98, 106, 123n. 34; humor, 90–91; minor characters, 90; origin, 86–88; religious aspects, 86–88, 92–93; response of reviewers, 86, 93; role of women, 89–90

NOVELS (*continued*)
Tall Houses in Winter, 11, 12, 13, 38, 39, 43, 61–65, 76, 78, 98; editorial problems, 38–39; major themes, 64; minor characters, 62; response of reviewers, 65; setting, 61; southern women, 62, 63–64
Who Is Sylvia?, 106
Wings of the Morning, 6, 106, 107

SHORT STORY COLLECTIONS
Astronomer and Other Stories, The, 11, 49–54, 79; "All That Glisters Isn't Gold," 8, 49, 51; "Astronomer, The," 49, 50, 51–53; "Careful, Sharp Eggs Under Foot," 49, 50–51; "Clarissa and the Depths," 49, 51, 110n. 16, 117n. 46; "Mandarin, The," 49, 50, 53; "Mule in the Yard," 51; "Proud and the Virtuous, The," 50, 117n. 44; "Spies in the Herb House, The," 9, 49, 51, 117n. 45
Beasts of the Southern Wild and Other Stories, 4, 22, 42, 43, 54–59, 70, 79; "Beasts of the Southern Wild," 55–56; "Benson Watts Is Dead and in Virginia," 56–57, 119n. 62; "Glory of His Nostrila, The," 118n. 58; "Mother-in-Law, The," 44, 54, 59, 95, 96; National Book Award nominee, 55; response of reviewers, 54–55; "Spider Gardens of Madagascar, The," 54; "Ugliest Pilgrim, The," 22, 31, 39, 57–58, 119n. 67; and *Violet* (film), 22, 58; and *Violet* (musical), 22, 58–59
Gentle Insurrection and Other Stories, The, 1, 11, 12, 38, 44–48, 60; "Family Album," 46; "First and Second Walls, The," 45; "Gentle Insurrection, The" (early title: "Yesterday Was the Last Time"), 45, 46; "Long, Long Day, The," 45; and *Mademoiselle* prize, 12, 44; "Mark of Distinction, A," 46, "Miss Parker Possessed," 46, 47–48; "Mr. Shawn and Father Scott," 12, 44, 48; "My Name Is Jacob," 45; "Our Feathered Friends," 45; response of reviewers, 45–46; "Serpents and Dove," 47; "Sword, The," 48; "Sympathetic Visitor, The" (early title: "A Crepe for Her Brother"), 11, 46, 48, 117n. 39; UNC-Putnam Prize, 1, 12, 13, 44–45; "Very Old Are Beautiful," 46

UNCOLLECTED STORIES
"End of Summer, The," 4
"Necromancer," 31–32
"Story of E, The," 31
"This Is the Only Time I'll Tell It," 106, 125n. 2

Betts, Lowry M. (husband), 12, 13, 23–24, 30, 56, 60
Brown, Rita Mae, 101
Buck, Pearl, 45

Capote, Truman, 48
Chapel Hill News, Betts as journalist at, 36
Cornwall, Patricia, *Postmortem,* 107
Cronin, Anthony, "Apology," 61–62

Davenport, Gary, 82–83

Eliot, T. S., 26, 51, 72
Ellison, Ralph, 48
Erskine, Albert, 48

Fadiman, Clifton, 78, 83
Faulkner, William, 41, 80, 85, 104 107; *The Sound and the Fury,* 65
Ferguson, Mary Anne, 28, 81
Freeze, John Guy (maternal grandfather), 3–4, 103

Gilchrist, Ellen, 107
Godwin, Gail, 107
Gordon, Mary, 32, 38
Graham, Billy, 26, 86, 87
Grau, Shirley Ann, 48, 79
Grumbach, Doris, 54

Hodges, Luther, 105

Jarrell, Randall, 11, 23

Kafka, Franz, 97; "Hunger Artist, The,"
    97; "Metamorphosis, The," 83
Kenan, Randall, 17, 18

Life, Betts as journalist at, 36
Lindberg, Stanley, 101

Mailer, Norman, 32
Masters, Hilary, 101, 102
McLaurin, Tim, 17, 18, 106–7
Milosz, Czeslaw, "With Her," 87
Moore, Marianne, 32

O'Connor, Flannery, 10, 15, 24–25, 26,
    27, 40–41, 48, 77, 80, 85, 100, 104,
    107; "Good Man Is Hard to Find, A,"
    83; "Revelation," 83; "View of the
    Woods, A," 68; *Wise Blood,*
    122n. 18

Paley, Grace, 32
Patton, Frances Gray, 11
Percy, Walker, 24, 27, 59, 104, 107
Porter, Katherine Anne, 11, 19
Prenshaw, Peggy W., 82
Price, Reynolds, 28, 107

Rawlings, Marjorie Kinnan, 45
Rehder, Jessie, 13, 45
Research Triangle Park, 104, 105, 106
Russell, Diarmuid, 42

Sanford Daily Herald, Betts as journalist
    at, 35–36
Sarton, May, 32
Scura, Dorothy, 44, 46, 49, 62, 83
Smith, Lee, 22, 101, 106
Statesville Daily Record, Betts as journalist
    at, 33–35
Steadman, Mark, 79
Street, James, 45

Taylor, Peter, 11, 48, 107
Thomas, Dylan, 4
Thompson, Francis, 88, 89; "Hound of
    Heaven, The," 88, 89, 92; "To Monica
    Thought Dying," 89
Tyler, Anne, 4, 42, 43, 54, 59, 107; *St.
    Maybe,* 49

Warren, Robert Penn, 11, 48, 80
Waugh, Mary Ellen Freeze (mother), 1, 3,
    4–5
Waugh, William Elmore (father), 1–2,
    4–5, 74
Welty, Eudora, 19, 28, 41, 42, 60, 85,
    104, 107; "A Worn Path," 67
Whitman, Walt, "When I Heard the
    Learn'd Astronomer," 52
Wilk, David, 101, 102

Yardley, Jonathan, 42, 54, 70, 81–82
Yourcenar, Marguerite, 107

The Author

Elizabeth Evans is the author of *Eudora Welty* (1981), *Thomas Wolfe* (1984), *May Sarton Revisited* (1989), and *Anne Tyler* (1993), all published by Twayne. Retired from the Georgia Institute of Technology, where she taught English, she lives in the mountains of western North Carolina.

The Editor

Frank Day is a professor of English and head of the English Department at Clemson University. He is the author of *Sir William Empson: An Annotated Bibliography* (1984) and *Arthur Koestler: A Guide to Research* (1985). He was a Fulbright lecturer in American literature in Romania (1980–1981) and in Bangladesh (1986–1987).